DPs Dominion
Publishing Services
http://www.dominionpublishingstores.yolasite.com

HORTICULTURAL MACHINERY
Operations & Safety

Segun R. Bello

B. Eng (Hons), FUT, Akure, MSc, Ibadan,
MNSE, MNIAE, FSINRHD, R. Engr. (COREN)

Horticultural machinery
Operations & safety

Copyright © 2013 by Segun R. Bello

Federal College of Agriculture Ishiagu, 480001 Nigeria
segemi2002@gmail.com; segemi2002@yahoo.com
http://www.dominionpublishingstores.yolasite.com
http://www.segzybrap.web.com
+234 8068576763, +234 8062432694

ISBN-13: 978- 148-497-487-2
      -10: 148-497-487-5

First Edition published in June 2013

Printed by Createspace US
7290 Investment Drive
Suite B North Charleston,
SC 29418 USA, www.createspace.com

This work is dedicated to

Moji, the love of my life

Acknowledgement

Glory is to God who gave strength to the meek and humble to do exploit. The author wish to express deep appreciations to students of the Department of Horticulture & Landscape Technology and the department of Agricultural Engineering Technology, Federal Colleges of Agriculture Ishiagu and Moor Plantation, Ibadan for their contributions during interactive class sessions and field discussions which has formed a major resource material in packaging this book.

The author wish to express deep appreciations to all students, trainees and technicians especially the students of agricultural and engineering technology in several institutions of learning across the nation who had increased in intellectual learning through contact with the outcome of my research activities Their meaningful contributions, feedbacks, criticisms and advice, comments and encouragements had contributed immensely to the putting together of this workbook.

The contributions and inputs of Engr. Ezebuilo C. N., and Okechukwu Omahi of the Department of Agricultural & Bio-Environmental Engineering Technology, Federal College of Agriculture, Ishiagu; Mr. Balogun R. B. of the Department, of Horticultural and Landscape Technology, Federal College of Agriculture, Ishiagu,; Engr. Adegbulugbe T. A. and Femi D. Aremu, of the Department, of Agricultural Engineering Technology, Federal College of Agriculture, Moor Plantation, Ibadan,; Engr. Odey Simon O., of the Agronomy Department, Cross River University of Technology, Obubra campus, Cross River State and other professional colleagues in associated institutions are immensely appreciated.

Despite all the help received from many people, it seems inevitable that there will be some inaccuracies or errors in the text. For these the author accepts responsibility and apologizes in advance for any incorrect statements or impressions given. Should errors be noticed, the author would welcome factual corrections. He would also be happy to receive comments, observations and additional information on any topic, section or statements in any part of the book. This would be particularly useful should any updated or translated edition be planned. Correspondence may be addressed to the author.

My sincere appreciation goes to all who at one point or the other, share my visions and mission. Your encouragements, unflinching supports and faithfulness will forever be acknowledged. The nudging from Ayomikun, 'Pelumi, Damilola, Adeola and Bukky are great impetus for the realization of this vision.

Content

Preface

Technological advancements and innovations in horticultural operations have revolutionized the age long profession and have in turn provided comfort and luxury for the operators and investors. This book is designed to provide the students with a good understanding of the various horticultural tools, description and areas of utilization in gardening and horticulture.

This book is packaged to provide the students with background knowledge of various horticultural operations, tool and equipment use. Written in simplified English with detailed graphic illustrations and pictures, the book is the perfect tool required in every home to in selecting tools and machines for horticultural and gardening operations.

The book is in five chapters: Chapter one providing background knowledge of horticulture and gardening, fields of professional qualification vocation and career opportunities.

Chapter two x-rays the various tools; its classifications, descriptions as well as areas of utilization.

Chapter three discussed gardening practices an operation including site selection, clearing, bed preparation, bed planting, plant tending, and fertilizer application as well as transplanting.

Chapter four takes a look at gardening power tools and machine; both driven and hand held covering various department of horticultural practice from cutting/pruning to harvest and packaging;. Their descriptions, utilization and operations were enumerated with high resolution graphics and sketches

Chapter five describes measure of safe tool and machine operation. Background knowledge of hazardous nature of tools and machines, safe selection and utilization as well as caring in form of maintenance and repairs fundamentals was presented in this chapter.

It is also designed to increase knowledge in students studying to acquire degrees and proficiency in certificate, diploma and higher levels of training in horticulture, agriculture and other related disciplines.

Bello, R. S.
480001, Nigeria

CHAPTER 1

HORTICULTURE & GARDENING

Content: Introduction to horticulture, aspects of horticulture and gardening, career opportunities in horticulture and gardening

1.   Introduction

Horticulture is an age long agricultural practice involved in the propagation, growing and caring for tree and garden crops, fruits and vegetables as well as ornamental plants for both pleasure and profit. Tree and garden crops are grown for food and fiber production while ornamental plants are often grown for their flowers, foliage, or overall appearance.

On the other hand, gardening is an aspect of horticulture involved in the the practice of growing and cultivation of plants. In gardens, useful plants, such as root vegetables, leafy vegetables, fruits, and herbs, are grown for consumption, for use as dyes, or for medicinal or cosmetic use.

Horticulture and gardening therefore involves the aesthetic cultivation of ornamental plants, native plants, fruits, vegetables, and flowers in public and domestic gardens as well as landscapes. They combine agriculture with environmental design, botany, and graphic arts.

1.1   Aspects of horticulture

There are several areas of professional study in horticulture industry, a few of them include:

Arboriculture

Arboriculture is concerned with the cultivation of trees or shrubs for scientific, commercial, or other purposes, especially for the production of timber. This is a practice as well as science involved in the management, and study of individual trees, shrubs, vines, and other perennial woody plants. Arboriculture is therefore related to, but distinct from agriculture, horticulture, forestry and silviculture in that arboriculture primarily focused on the maintenance of individual woody plants and trees, usually in gardens, parks or other populated settings for permanent landscape, amenity, enjoyment, protection, purposes for the benefit of man.

The science of arboriculture studies how these plants grow and respond to cultural practices and to their environment. The practice of arboriculture includes cultural techniques such as selection, planting, training, fertilization, pest and pathogen control, pruning, shaping, and removal.

Market gardening

Market garden refers to the relatively small-scale production of fruits, vegetables and flowers as cash crops, frequently sold directly to consumers and restaurants. It is distinguishable from other types of farming by the diversity of crops grown on a small area of land, typically, from under one acre (0.4hA) to a few acres, or sometimes in greenhouses. Such a farm on a larger scale is sometimes called a truck farm.

A market garden is a business based on provision of wide range and steady supply of fresh produce through the local growing season. Many different crops and varieties are grown, in contrast with large, industrialized farms, which tend to specialize in high volume production of single crops, a practice known as monoculture.

Orchards

An orchard is an intentional planting of trees or shrubs that is maintained for food production. Orchards comprise fruit or nut-producing trees which are grown for commercial production. Orchards are also sometimes a feature of large gardens, where they serve an aesthetic as well as a productive purpose.

Floriculture

Floriculture includes the cultivation or production and marketing of flowering and ornamental plants especially for ornamental purposes. It is a branch of ornamental horticulture concerned with growing and marketing flowers and ornamental plants, as well as flower arrangement. It is also described as a segment of horticulture concerned with commercial production, marketing, and retail sale of cut flowers and potted plants, as well as home gardening and flower arrangement.

Amenity horticulture

Amenity horticulture otherwise known as turf management includes all aspects of the production and maintenance of turf grass for sports, leisure use or amenity use. It is all about changing the environment in home gardens, street gardens, parks and rural settings to make them more pleasant and practical to live in.

Nurseries

A nursery is a place where plants are propagated and grown to usable size. They include retail nurseries which sell to the general public, wholesale nurseries which sell only to businesses such as other nurseries and to commercial gardeners, and private nurseries which supply the needs of institutions or private estates.

Landscape horticulture

Landscape horticulture includes the production, marketing and maintenance of landscape plants. Aspects of landscape horticulture include landscape design & landscape construction which is involved with the changing of outdoor environment to make it more users friendly. The change can be to make the area both visually attractive and physically more useable and manageable. Landscape design has two major components along which they were developed:

- Soft features made up of plants
- Hard features that are non-living structures such as patios, decks, swimming pools, children's play equipment, conservatories, pergolas, paths and drives, steps, walls, fences, outdoor furniture, interest features, ponds and fountains. Part of the reason for landscaping includes

Other areas of horticultural study

Other areas of horticultural study include

- *Pomology* includes the production and marketing of pome fruits.
- *Viticulture* includes the production and marketing of grapes.
- *Oenology* includes all aspects of wine and winemaking.
- *Postharvest physiology* involves maintaining the quality of and preventing the spoilage of horticultural crops.

1.2   Aspects of gardening

Different aspects of gardening ranges in scale from fruit orchards, to long boulevard plantings with one or more different types of shrubs, trees and herbaceous plants, to residential yards including lawns and foundation plantings, to plants in large or small containers grown inside or outside. Gardening may be very specialized, with only one type of plant grown, or involve a large number of different plants in mixed plantings. The following gardening practices are common;

Residential gardening: This takes place near the home, in a space referred to as the garden. Although a garden typically is located on the land near a residence, it may also be located on a roof, or on a balcony. Gardening also takes place in non-residential green areas, such as parks, public or semi-public gardens (botanical gardens or zoological gardens), amusement and amusement parks.

Indoor gardening is concerned with the growing of houseplants within a residence or building, in a conservatory, or in a greenhouse. Indoor gardens are sometimes incorporated as part of air conditioning or heating systems.

Native plant gardening is concerned with the use of native plants with or without the intent of creating wildlife habitat. The goal is to create a garden in harmony with, and adapted to a given area. This type of gardening typically reduces water usage, maintenance, and fertilization costs, while increasing native faunal interest.

Water gardening is concerned with growing plants adapted to pools and ponds. These all require special conditions and considerations. A simple water garden may consist solely of a tub containing the water and plant(s). In aquascaping, a garden is created within an aquarium tank.

Container gardening is concerned with growing plants in any type of container either indoors or outdoors. Common containers are pots, hanging baskets, and planters. Container gardening is usually used in atriums and on balconies, patios, and roof tops.

Community gardening is a social activity in which an area of land is gardened by a group of people, providing access to fresh produce and plants as well as access to satisfying labor, neighborhood improvement, sense of community and connection to the environment .Community gardens are typically owned in trust by local governments or nonprofits.

1.3   Career opportunities in horticulture and gardening

Horticulturists can work in industry, government or educational institutions or private collections. They can be cropping systems engineers, wholesale or retail business managers, propagators and tissue culture specialists (fruits, vegetables, ornamentals, and turf), crop inspectors, crop production advisers, extension specialists, plant breeders, research scientists, and teachers.

CHAPTER 2

GARDENING TOOLS & SELECTION

Contents: Introduction to gardening tools, classification of gardening tools, gardening tools description, selection and utilization

2. Introduction

To retain the beauty of horticultural garden or farm, you need to put in commensurate efforts that require time, money and energy. The right tools and right attitude are functions of money and time while energy involvement will make horticultural project easy and quicker to accomplish. Having the right tools, knowing how to use them and management decisions relating to the selection of horticultural tools and equipment, choice of practice, market availability, and availability of storage facilities among others are essential factors can affect horticultural operations and production profits in several ways.

Figure 2-1: Horticultural tools

To improve productivity and efficiency, it is necessary to have comprehensive knowledge of horticultural tools and implement performance as well as horticultural crop processing and preservation.

Owing to the ever increasing demands of horticultural industry relating to use of precision tools and other hardware, efforts toward design of tools to provide maximum output and ease of usage, has become very popular. Today with the increased technological knowledge, there are multi-variant equipments that can handle horticultural operations such trimming or cutting grass in a lawn, garden or farm.

2.1 Gardening tools and classification

Today, vegetable gardening tools are bulk-produced for sale and easily attained at your local home improvement and garden center, but at one time in our history (and now in many developing countries) gardening tools were highly prized, and crucial for the livelihood of a family.

Gardening tools are working aids used to manually carry out gardening tasks such as trimming, pruning, bushing, transplanting, removing weeds, digging soil and aerating soil. Gardening range of tools is made for gardening, agriculture and horticultural operations. Common gardening tools include shovels, spades, trowels, rakes, hoes, tillers, shears and saws.

Classification of garden tools

Garden tools can be classified into two categories as either hand held tools or power driven tools. Limited spaced gardening often requires short-handled tools in order not to disrupt plantings when you are cultivating under low perennials, weeding around thorny or prickly specimens, or working tough soil where you need some serious leverage. There are many short-handled hand-held tools from which to choose. Some of these tools are considered in the following sections.

2.2 Hand held gardening tools and description

The hand held tools used by gardeners originated with the earliest agricultural implements used by man which include the spade, garden hoe, pitchfork, garden fork, garden rake and the plough among several others.

Figure 2-2: Garden tools

The earliest forms of garden tools were made of wood, flint and bone. The development of metal working, first in copper and later in iron and steel, enabled the manufacturing of stronger and more durable tools. Industrial revolution in metalworking had enabled the development and sophistication of garden tools. Hand held gardening tools can be broadly categorized and described under the followings sub headings:

1. Digging tools
2. Clearing tools
3. Trimming, pruning and thinning tools
4. Harvest tools
5. Plant protection tools
6. Products carts

2.2.1 Digging tools and description

Spade and shovel

A spade is a tool designed primarily for the purpose of digging or loosening and removal of earth and spreading it evenly where required. Garden spade is an essential tool for double-digging food growing beds. It has a flat blade with sharp edges which can both break and move the earth under most stringent situations as well as increase efficiency.

Types of spade

- *Flat edge garden spade:* Flat edge spade forms one of the chief implements wielded by the hand in agriculture and horticultural operations. It is sometimes considered a type of shovel. The typical shape of spade is a broad flat blade with a sharp lower edge, straight or curved. The upper edge on either side of the handle affords space for the user's foot, which drives it into the ground. The wooden handle ends in a cross-piece, sometimes T-shaped and sometimes forming a kind of loop in form of letter 'D' for the hand.

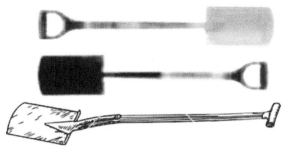

Figure 2-3: Digging spades

- *Garden round point shovel:* Shovels are hand tools consisting of a broad blade fixed to a medium-length handle. Shovel blades are usually made of sheet steel or hard plastics and are very strong. Shovel handles are usually made of wood or glass-reinforced plastic (fiberglass).

  Two types of shovels are in use in home garden; both having long handles and are used when you are standing up;

  - *Garden round point shovel* is a "must have" universal garden tool which has a rounded, sharp edge on the blade, making it suitable for digging into hard soil.

Figure 2-4: Garden round point shovel

  - Square-shaped shovels act like a scoop and are used to move already loosened soil from one area of the garden to another.

Figure 2-5: Square shaped shovel

Uses: A shovel is a tool for digging, lifting, and moving bulk materials, such as soil, coal, gravel, sand.Used in garden planting operations. It can also be used to scrap or weed annual weeds at ground level.

Crowbar

The crowbar is a hand tool fabricated from an octagonal bar. One of the ends is pointed and the other is spoon or chiselled shaped. The spoon or chiselled shape end is either forged from the bar or separately made and welded to the end of crow bar. The crow bar is made either from the structural steel or from medium carbon steel. The crow bar ends are forged to shape and hardened to 350-400 HB. For its operation, t he tool is held in both hands in vertical position and driven into the soil by impact

Figure 2-6: Crowbars

Uses: For digging holes or pits for planting and fencing

Garden fork

Description: A garden fork is an implement, with a handle and several (usually four) sturdy and strong tines. Garden forks have short, wooden handle, with a "D" or "T" end. Garden forks were originally made of wood, but the majorities are now made of carbon steel or stainless steel. Their tines are usually shorter, flatter, thicker, and more closely spaced.

Figure 2-7: Garden forks

Garden forks are slightly shorter and thicker than pitch forks. The strongest have square, rather than flat tines.

Uses: Digging fork is an ideal tool for turning and cultivating soil. It is used for general loosening the second layer of double-digging, lifting and turning over soil in gardening operations as well as for moving mulch, sod, and debris. It can also be used to aerate the top layer of your beds during the growing season before subsequent crops, to rake out stones and weeds and break up clods.

Functional requirements

1. The tines allow the implement to be pushed more easily into the ground,
2. It can take out stones and weeds and break up clods,
3. It is not so easily stopped by stones, and
4. It does not cut through weed roots or root-crops.

Pitchforks

Description: Pitchfork is an agricultural tool with a long handle and long, thin, widely separated pointed tines (also called prongs). They are usually made of steel with a long wooden handle, but may also be made from wood, wrought iron, bamboo, alloy etc. Pitchforks typically have only three or four tines

Figure 2-8: Pitchforks forks

Uses: Used to lift and pitch (throw) loose material, such as piled hay, compost, or manure or leaves.

Border fork or *ladies' fork*

Description: Border fork is a smaller fork with shorter but a full-sized handle, closer-spaced, thinner tines. The tine designs include broad flat tines and back-to-back forks design.

Figure 2-9: Border forks

Uses: Designed for lighter work such as cleaning up and weeding border areas as well as thinning vegetables and perennials. Forks with broader, flatter tines are made for lifting potatoes and other root crops from the ground. A pair of forks back-to-back is often used to lever apart dense clumps of roots.

Dung *fork*

Description: Dung forks dung forks have four or five slim tines with long handles made of wood.

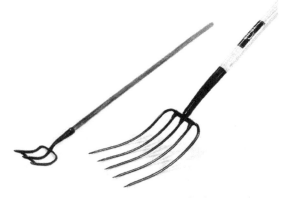

Figure 2-10: Dung forks

Uses: The dung fork was used to work manure into the earth.

Hand fork

Description: A hand fork is an implement, with a comparatively short wooden handle with round end and usually three sturdy and strong but sharp tines. a hand fork is easy to stab into the soil (most soil) making it great for planting, transplanting, aerating, weeding and mixing additives into your soil.

Figure 2-11: Hand forks

Uses: The hand fork makes a good all-around garden tool, especially in tight places. It is used to turn manure into the earth.

Hand operated aerator

Description: Hand operated aerator is a bed/soil preparation tool has 8 spikes each having a thickness of between 9½-11 inches, a 14 inches weight tray, 14" spiking width and 7/8" wheel diameter x 17 ¼ " axle and weighs up to 30 lbs.

Figure 2-12: Hand operated aerator

Uses: Hand operated aerator is used to aerate lawns and small yards without the use of a tractor.

Tractor operated spike aerator

Description: The trail behind aerator bed/soil preparations implement has such features as 36" spiking width, 18 spikes each having a thickness of between 9½-11 inches. The depth of penetration is controlled by the amount of ballast added to the weight tray. The aerator has 6" diameter transport wheels and weighs up to 70 lbs.

Figure2-13: Hand operated aerator

Uses: Tractor operated spike aerator can be used with any tractor with a draw bar to aerate lawns and large yards.

Hand trowel

Description: Trowels are hand held gardening tools with a pointed, scoop-shaped metal blade and a short plastic or wooden handle made from pressed steel. This handheld shovel comes with a variety of blade shapes and lengths but all have a rounded, sharp point to make piercing the soil easier. A narrow blade is good for digging in solid soil. Wide, rounded blades remove soil faster.

Figure 2-14: Hand trowels

The choice of hand trowel depends on ergonomic design considerations which include

- *Choice of materials:* Steel blades will last longer while soft rubber handles are easier on the grip but easily get damaged.
- *Stress:* Most planting exercise will require you get down on your knees when using a trowel, however, some ergonomic designed trowels assist in taking stress off of your wrist while in use.

Uses: Hand trowel allows you to

a. Quickly dig planting holes for seeds or seedlings.
b. Break up earth, digging small holes, especially for planting, weeding, mixing in fertilizer or other additives, and
c. Transferring plants to pots and seedlings to the field.

Hand scoop

Description: These are solid, one-piece casting tools designed for use in the garden, kitchen or farm shop. They are built for strength, sturdy and not easily broken down (high reliability). The smallest size of the tool has a scoop size of 4 ½" long and 2 ¾" wide, the middle scoop a size of 6 x 3¼" and the largest a size of 7 ¾" long and 4½" wide.

Figure 2-15: Hand trowels

Uses: Some typical uses of h*and scoop* include scooping up of fireplace ashes and potting soil.

Double ended hand digger

Description: Double ended hand digger is a durable, aggressive digging tool with working head 10 inches long having a wide weighty flat pick and a narrow pointed pick at opposite ends. The handle is about 14" in length made of wood. Wooden-handled hand diggers are attractive but ultimately too light for effective use.

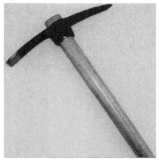

Figure 2-16: Garden digger

Uses: This garden tool is used for picking and digging out stones, roots and stubble.

Garden axe

Description: Garden axe is a finely tempered and highly tuned top notch cutting tool with long wooden handle and flat cutting edge. The cutting edge can be wide or narrow depending on choice of operation. The wideness of the head provides a longer striking surface than other narrow headed axes and therefore helps ensure good swing when striking solid wood. The striking head is forged and slightly thicker just behind the leading cutting edge but thins out slightly afterwards, thus reducing "wedging" pressure and enhancing penetration.

Figure 2-17: Garden axe

Garden axe are in two categories include:

Limbing axe: The limbing axe is approximately 25 inches long and weighs 3 lbs.

Felling axe: The felling axe is longer in length than the limbing axe, about 29 inches long and weighs 4¼ lbs. The butt end opposite from the cutting edge (called the poll) of the felling axe is tempered so that this tool can also be used as a striking maul.

Uses: Garden axes are generally used for felling trees, cutting out roots and other activities involving cutting and chipping out in the garden.

Mattocks

Description: Mattock is a digging tool with a flat blade set at right angles to the handle. It is like a pickaxe but has a flat, adz-shaped blade on one or both sides.

Figure 2-18: Garden mattock

Uses: Mattock tools are used for loosening soil, digging up and cutting roots, etc. Mattock is also used to strip turf and break up hard pan or ground and a spade to dig out the earth.

Various designs of mattock are available for varying degree of use and these include:

Cutter mattock

The cutter mattock head is made from forged steel, weighing about 5-pounds and features two metal heads, one end in hoe blade and the other end in cutter blade.

Figure 2-19: Cutter mattock

The forged steel structure ensures ultimate durability and safety. This head endures the constant pounding from digging up roots and breaking hardened soil.

Figure 2-20: Cutter mattock head

Features

a. Ideal for digging trenches, breaking up hard soil, and cutting roots
b. The forged steel head is good for durability and safety when fracturing compacted soil
c. Features two heads of metal, one end hoe blade, and the other ends in cutter blade.

Mattock pickaxe

Description: This strong mattock pickaxe is made from forged steel and features two heads of metal, with a pointed end and a flat end.

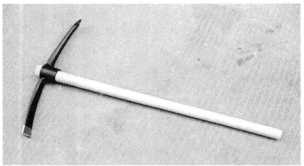

Figure 2-21: Pickaxe mattock

The steel head is heat treated, durable, and painted black. The handle is made with a rugged hardwood for strength and durability

Figure 2-22: Pickaxe mattock heads

Features

a. It is ideal for breaking up hard, rocky soil
b. The drop- forged steel head is designed for durability and safety when fracturing compacted soil
c. Features two heads of metal, one end chisel, and one end pick point

Uses: The principal use of this tool is to break rock surfaces, concrete, or dried soil.

Railroad pickaxe

Description: This is a strong mattock pickaxe made from forged steel and features two heads of metal, with a pointed end and a flat end. The steel head is heat treated, durable, and painted black with a rugged hardwood handle

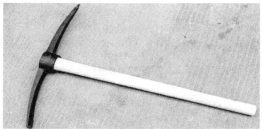
Figure 2-23: Railroad pickaxe

Features

a. Hardwood handle is 36-inch long with a handle guard to provide permanent protection
b. Heavy duty double forged head features a mattock
c. Rugged wooden handle will withstand repeated striking.

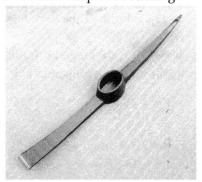
Figure 2-24: Railroad pickaxe head

Uses: The key features this tool is ideal to break and rupturing rock surfaces, concrete, or hardened dried soil. It is also ideal for planting, tilling, ground preparation, and cultivating

2.2.2 Garden clearing tools and description

Clearing tools most commonly found in use in gardening and orchard operations include weeders, hoe, rakes, sweepers, dusters etc. Some of these tools and equipments are considered below.

Garden weeders

Gardening operation is physically demanding involving kneeling down and/or bending forward while weeding, planting or harvesting. To overcome such job demand, different weeder tools and equipment have been developed which allows workers to tend the crops. Few examples were described below

Hand cultivator

Description: Hand cultivators have a short wooden handle, 10 to 11 inches long with 3 to 5 forged steel claw tines to match desired jobs. The hand claw tools vary in size and are suitable for gardening operations.

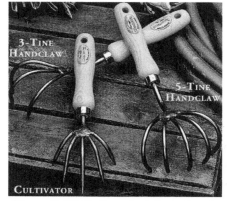

Figure2-25: Railroad pickaxe head

Uses: Hand cultivators are suitable tools for digging and pulling loose soil toward self. The 5-tine cultivator excels at pushing soil around - shaping and smoothing.

Weed extractor

Description: This is a simple, effortless tool invented in 1913, and was very efficiently used until World War II halted its production but now rediscovered after 70 years. It comprises of a long wooden handle and a picker head.

The picker head has two iron gripping prongs that opens and closes when the footpad lever is operated. In operation, it extracts weed in just two simple operations as described below:

Step 1: Simply center the two iron gripping prongs over the weed (footpad lever can point in either direction), press into the ground

Figure 2-26: Step 1-Setting and pressing down

Step 2: Remove your foot, leaning the 39" long hardwood handle in the direction of the footpad lever, and then pull out the whole weed, root and all.

Figure 2-26: Step 2-Bending and pulling out

Uses: It is used in effortless plant extraction and weeding-without bending, hand pulling, or kneeling down.

Triple-claw weeder

Description: Triple-claw weeder makes it easy to remove invasive plants from lawn without kneeling, bending over or using harsh, costly herbicides.

The durable steel handle is extra-long to help reach every weed without kneeling or straining your back by bending.

Figure 2-27: Triple-claw weeders

It features includes three serrated, stainless-steel claws that grab weeds by the root for clean removal, plus an easy-eject mechanism on the handle that clears the head between uses without forcing you to bend over and remove it by hand.

Figure2-28: Stainless-steel claws

In operation, the claw head has two iron gripping prongs that opens and closes when the footpad lever is operated.

Figure 2-29: Triple-claw weeder display extracted weed

The tool extracts weed in just two simple operations as described below:

Step 1: Simply center the two iron gripping prongs over the weed (footpad lever can point in either direction), press into the ground

Figure 2-30: Step 1-Setting and pressing down

Step 2: Remove your foot, leaning the 39" long hardwood handle in the direction of the footpad lever, and then pull out the whole weed, root and all.

Figure2-31: Step 2-Bending and pulling out

Uses: Ideal for removing dandelions, thistles and other invasive weeds without kneeling, bending or using harsh, costly herbicide.

Wunda Weeder

Description: The device which was invented and used in Australia is a four-wheeled metal frame, with a stretcher-like bed on the bottom, and a sunshade/rain cover and solar panel assembly on top. For wind protection, or if the sunlight or rain are coming in at an angle, there are side shades that can be lowered.

Figure 2-32: Wunda weeder on display

The user lies face-down on the bed, with forehead on an adjustable headrest, and their arms free to dangle down and toil in the row of plants below. The bed's elevation can be adjusted, depending on the crop and the activity. When the user wants to move ahead, they just use a hand lever to activate the solar-powered electric motor, which can also go in reverse. To move the device from one area to another, the user can walk behind it while still operating the motor, via its "walk switch."

Figure2-33: Wunda weeder on display

Garden hoes

Description: A garden hoe is a hand-held tool with tined head, wide or narrow metal plate (depending on choice) fixed to a (long or short) wooden, plastic or metal handle used to move small amounts of soil in gardening or weeding operations. The handle can be short or long depending on choice and convenience.

Figure 2-34: Garden hoes

Handheld versions work well for weeding close to desirable plants, while long-handled hoes allow you to quickly clear the area between rows of plants.

Figure 2-35: Combined garden hoe and fork

Uses: Garden hoe is used to soften and break up the top soil up to 4 inches deep into the earth. Related functional use include weed control by agitating the surface of the soil around plants, piling soil around the base of plants (hilling), creating narrow furrows (drills) and shallow trenches for planting seeds and bulbs, to chop weeds, roots and crop residues, and even to dig or move soil, such as when harvesting root crops like potatoes.

Rakes

Description: Rake is an implement consisting of a toothed bar fixed transversely to a long or short handle depending on the choice of operation. They come in a variety of sizes and tine strength. Some typical rake tooth bar designs were shown in figure below

Tines with some spring can be used in the garden without too much damage to plants. A narrow rake can maneuver around plants easier, but a wide rake makes quicker work of leaves. As with trowels, many rakes now come with ergonomic handles that put less stress on your back.

Figure 3-36: Rake tooth bars

Uses: Rakes are primarily used prior to planting or during end-of-season cleanup. Rakes are used to collect leaves, hay, grass, etc., and, in gardening, for loosening the soil, light weeding and leveling, removing dead grass from lawns, and generally for purposes performed in agriculture by the harrow. Rubber rakes are good for raking debris from around delicate plants.

Types of rakes

There are several kinds of garden rakes, usually specific to the job at hand, such as:

Garden bow rake: Garden bow rake is used to even out growing beds and to help rake out loose soil clods and organic stubble.

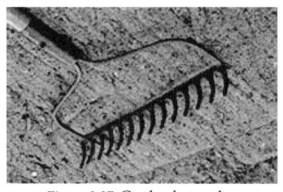

Figure 2-37: Garden bow rake

Long-handle rakes: Long-handle rakes come in a variety of types for different purposes, but have one thing in common…saving your back from constant bending.

Figure 2-38: Long-handle rakes

Short handled rakes: Short handled rakes do the same work as the larger versions, but are more effective when raking in confined spaces such as in between plantings. They give excellent results when used in clearing debris from beds.

Figure 2-39: Short handle rakes

Small hand rakes with sturdy tines can be used to clear or help loosen the soil in small areas.

Leaf rakes: This has leaf-like tooth bar which are excellent for cleaning leaves and rubbish along the lawn.

Figure 2-40: Leaf rake

Garden rakes: Garden rakes have short stiff steel tines are great for leveling dirt or breaking up dirt clumps

Figure 2-41: Garden rake

Heavy metal rake: These are long and straight with teeth about 3" long. They are necessary to smooth out newly tilled garden soil and break up clumps.

2.2.3 Plant protection tools and description

Plant protection tools and equipment includes chemical applicators (dusters for spraying dry chemicals, spraying equipments for liquid chemicals), fertilizer applicators and watering can etc.

Spraying equipment for liquid chemicals

Spraying equipment include hand held sprayers, and equipment for weed controls

- *Hand held sprayers:* Most hand sprayers in these sizes use compressed air for pressurizing the supply tank and have adjustable handguns or wands. Hand held sprayers are built to meet such features as safety, comfort, durability, ease of maintenance and economy.

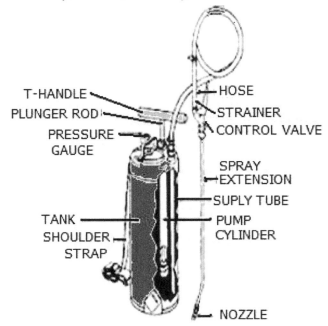

Figure 2-42: Hand sprayers

Standard specification includes: automatic chemical agitation, unique trigger safety valve, seals, external pressure control, comfortable back rest, professional nozzles, lance storage clip, 'safe guard' tank, visible fluid level, telescopic lance, carrying handle, pressure gauge, wide straps and waist belt.

Uses: Manual hand sprayers are designed for spot treatments and for restricted areas unsuitable for larger units. Hand sprayers are generally used on small areas; therefore, the amount of spray applied should be calculated for small areas.

i. *Backpack/knapsack sprayers:* Although labour-intensive, backpack or knapsack sprayers are relatively light and can be taken to places where mounted sprayers are difficult to use.

Figure 2-43: Knapsack sprayer

Most backpack sprayers come in 3- or 4-gallon sizes. They work well in small orchards, lawns or small fruit garden areas. Backpack sprayers are either manually operated or engine-powered.

ii. *Battery-operated hand sprayer:* Battery-powered controlled droplet applicators (CDA) use a spinning disk type of atomizer to produce a uniform droplet size. These units are suitable for ultra low volume (ULV) applications.

Figure 2-44: Controlled droplet applicator

Thus the amount of material that must be carried by the operator is greatly reduced. The droplet size is inversely proportional to the disk RPM. The units are lightweight, easy to use and usually powered with common flashlight dry cells; the batteries being positioned in the handle

iii. *Motorised sprayers:* These sprayers are equipped with a two-stroke gasoline engine to build up enough pressure in the liquid tank. The entire unit is mounted on human back.

Figure 2-45: Motorised sprayers

iv. *Boom sprayers*: Boom sprayers are commonly used for low growing crops because the boom can extend outward and over the crop (Figure 2-46). They can also be used in maintaining the floor of orchards where herbicides can eliminate or control the growth of ground cover on the orchard floor. Boom sprayers can be tractor-mounted or self-propelled.

Figure 2-47: Boom sprayer

v. *Hydraulic handgun sprayers*: Hydraulic handgun sprayers are hand-held gun sprayers that can spray pesticide into the tops of fruit and shade trees (Figure 2-48). Water or oil is used as both the diluents and the carrier. The sprayer must provide and maintain high pressure and sufficient flow of liquid so that the large droplets of the stream can reach the tops of the trees.

Figure 2-48: Hydraulic handgun sprayer

vi. *Airblast sprayers*: Airblast sprayers use a high-velocity, large-volume airstream to apply a concentrated pesticide mixture (Figure 2-49). Airblast sprayers can be one-way (one-sided) or two-way (two-sided). These types of sprayers are not commonly found or readily available now.

Figure 2-49: Airblast sprayer

Spraying equipment for dry chemicals

Equipment typically used in dry chemical application is the duster. Depending on the source of power, dusters can be classified into manually operated types and power operated types.

a.   Manually operated dusters

Manually operated dusters include; (i) package duster (ii) plunger duster (iii) bellows duster (iv) knapsack duster and (v) rotary duster.

i.   *Package dusters*: Pesticide dusts are packed in containers that serve as hand applicators which may be discarded after use. They are mostly provided with rubber, leather or plastic section which, on squeezing, provides a puff of air that emits the dust in a small cloud. The simplest type of package duster is worked by pressing it between the fingers. These include thee shake types, flick types, plastic squeeze type and the plunger carton types.

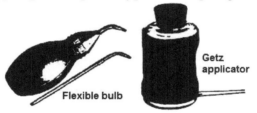

Figure 2-50: Package dusters

ii.   *Plunger dusters*: The consists of an air pump of the simple plunger type, a dust chamber, and a discharge assembly consisting of a straight tube or a small exit pipe whose discharge outlet can be increased or decreased by moving a lid provided at the end of the dust chamber.

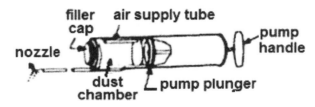

Figure 2-51: Plunger type duster

The air from the pump is directed through a tube into the container where it agitates the dust and ejects it from a discharge orifice or tube. The amount of dust can be controlled by the speed of the operation of the pump. These are useful for spot application in restricted areas and for controlling ants, poultry pest and pest of farm animals.

iii. *Bellows duster*: The bellows duster may be made from rubber, leather or plastic and has an adjustable plastic extension lance. On squeezing, it puffs the air that expels the dust in a small cloud. Hand held bellows duster has containers of capacity from 30 g to 500 g. The bellows can be operated either directly by hand or by handle provided for that purpose.

Figure 2-52: Bellows type duster

The duster is perfect for use with diatom powder for the control of red mite and insects inside the poultry houses and also ideal for use in gardens for accurate spraying of herbicides and pesticides on plants and crops. It is also a great tool for use in the home when spraying flea and insect control powders.

iv. *Knapsack duster*: The knapsack duster has the container capacity of 2.5 to 5.0 kg. The air blast developed by the bellow draws the dust from the hopper and discharges through the delivery spout intermittently. These dusters are suitable for spot treatments.

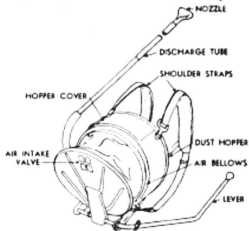

Figure 2-53: Knapsack type duster

v. *Rotary (crank) duster:* A Rotary duster consists basically of a blower complete with a gear box and a hopper. It is operated by rotating the crank. The cranking motion is transmitted through the gear box to the blower. A drive is taken for the dust agitator located in the hopper.

Figure 3-54: Rotary duster

The rotary duster may be hand carried type or shoulder mounted or belly carried type. The shoulder mounted type hand rotary dusters range consists basically of blower complete with gear box and hopper joined together by a suction pipe. The feed is controlled by a feed control lever, which operates a slide to control the aperture at the bottom of the hopper.

Figure 2-55: Shoulder mounted rotary duster

These rotary dusters are useful for continuous treatment of medium and smallholdings of cereals, pulses, groundnut, cotton, tobacco, potato, and vegetable crops. Shoulder mounted type hand rotary duster is used for dusting pesticides in powder form.

b. *Power operated dusters*

This resembles the rotary duster in construction, except that the power to drive the blower through the gear box is tapped from an external power source which may be an engine or P.T.O. shaft of tractor or flywheel of a power tiller. The power operated centrifugal energy knapsack sprayer also can be converted into a power duster, by allowing the dust fluid into the air stream, near the point of attaching the pleated hose, in the blower elbow.

Figure 2-56: Wheelbarrow duster

Aerial dust application: Dry powdery chemicals can also be applied to large hectrage of land through small agricultural aircrafts flying at low altitudes and close to the vegetation/crops. This is particularly suitable for orchard and plantation use.

Figure 2-57: Aerial application of chemical

Watering cans

Description: A watering can (or watering pot) is a portable container made of lightweight metal or plastic with a handle and detachable spout through which water and other liquid content can be applied in showers (tiny droplets) to young plants in nursery or directly on the field by hand. The capacity of the container varies from 0.5 liters for use with household plants to 10 liters for general garden use.

Figure 2-58: Watering can

A good watering can will have a handle that balances in your hand. Handles that curve from the front of the can to the bottom make it easier to tilt.

Uses: Watering can is used in adding water to garden plants and also used in soil preparation in the nursery.

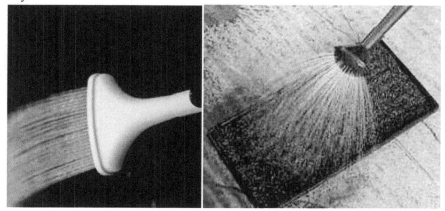

Figure 2-59: Watering can spout spray

Watering hoses

Description: These are long rubber tubing with varying diameters and length used as channels through which water is distributed around the garden from a source. Quality of water hose is determined by

- *Burst strength*: Burst strength is described as how much pressure a hose can handle before it bursts open. 50 pounds per sq. inch burst strength is a good strength.
- *Quantity of water flow*: The wider the hose, Burst strength the more water can flow through it. ½ inch is fine, but 5/8 inch is better.
- *Weather resistance*: Rubber will withstand the weather better, but the important thing is that whatever the material, it bee reinforced with a mesh layer.

2.2.4 Garden cutter tools and description

Garden cutting operations include trimming, pruning, grafting, girdling and thinning. These operations require specialized tools with carefully designed curves and shape patterns. Some examples of these cutter tools are described below.

Garden cutter (shares) tools

Description: Garden cutters such as thinning scissors and lawn shears have ergonomically designed hollow lightweight polypropylene handles for comfort and ease of use. The blades are designed in different shapes and forms for specific operation and for lasting sharpness

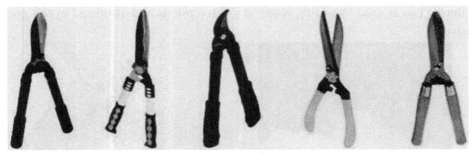

Figure 3-60: Garden shares

Uses: Garden cutters are used for trimming plant heads and reducing overgrown hedges.

Horticultural/craft scissors

Description: Horticultural/craft scissors are general purpose scissors made from 7cm high long carbon steel blades, ergonomic aluminum handles and blade sheath

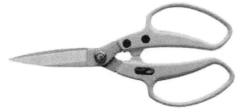

Figure 2-61: Horticultural/craft scissors

Uses: The general purpose scissors is used for horticulture/craft/harvest cut up to 10mm floral stems

Grass shear

Description: Grass shear is a professional shear with 135mm polished high carbon steel blade designed for 3 versatile positions: vertical for edging; horizontal for trimming; angled for hard to reach areas. There is an adjustable spring used to tension the top blade. The handles are hard chrome plated with non-slip grips with ease of setting the thumb lock.

Figure 2-62: Grass shear (Barnel B5050)

Uses: grass share is used for grass edging, trimming and angle cuts etc.

Edging knife

Description: This traditional cutting tool with blade made from stainless metal and a long handle making it very comfortable to use

Uses: Edging knife is used for weeding between paving bricks/rocks

Figure 2-63: Edging knife

Edging shovel

Description: Edging shovel is a sharp stainless blade which cuts through turf with ease and will make an impressive addition to any lawn-loving gardener's shed

Figure 2-64: Edging shovel

Uses: Edging shovel is used for cutting through turf and lawn

Pruning tools

Pruning simply implies deadheading and shaping of plants in the garden. Good pruners make a cleaner cut on the plants and not tear or rip the plant. Hand pruning tools for brushing and pruning includes pruning saw, *secateurs,* sickles, and pruning knives.

There are three different blade designs for pruning shears: *anvil, bypass* and *parrot-beak.*

Anvil pruners: Anvil pruners have only one blade, which closes onto a flat surface. They tend to crush the stem, but remain reliable when they are slightly blunt. Anvil secateurs are useful for cutting thick branches.

Bypass pruners: Bypass secateurs usually work exactly like a pair of scissors, with two blades passing each other to make the cut. At least one of the blades will be curved: a convex upper blade with either a concave or straight lower one. Some bypass designs have only one blade, the lower jaw being broad (like an anvil) but passing the upper jaw.

Figure 2-65: Bypass secateurs

Parrot-beak pruners: Parrot-beak secateurs consist of two concave passing blades, which trap the stem between them to make the cut. These are suitable only for narrower stems.

In making a choice of pruners, look for pruners with replaceable parts and blades that can be sharpened.

Long reach pruner

When gardening, one often finds that one's arms are simply too short to reach some designated places, even while picking or punning relatively small trees or climbing trees, one has to reach out to those places by climbing up a ladder - with all the risks that can entail on soft ground.

Pole pruner

With a pole pruner, one can extend one's reach by 1.5 meters (5 feet) or 3 meters (10 feet) depending on type. With a telescoping pole, and the various heads designed for it, one can reach up more than 5 meters (17 feet) while keeping one's feet on solid ground.

Description: Long reach pole pruner has an extendable pole capable of reaching up to 3 meters length and delivered with 240 mm saw blade.

Figure 2-66: Long reach pole pruner

The toothed anvil, or back, holds the branch firmly in place as the blade snaps. The minimum length is 1450 mm extendable to 3000 mm with the blade length measuring 55 mm and shears for branches up to 10 mm diameter. The tool weighs 1400 g.

Uses: The pole pruner is not only useful with high branches, but also allows one to keep a comfortable distance when pruning thorny trees and bushes. One can comfortably cut branches up to 10 mm in diameter once in areas reachable only by ladder.

Pole pruner head

Description: This anvil-pole shears pole pruner is specially designed with anvil for cutting dead and dried-out branches. The minimum length is 1450 mm extendable to 3000 mm with the blade length measuring 55 mm and shears for branches up to 15 mm diameter. The tool weighs 1400 g.

Figure 2-67: Anvil-pole shears

Uses: Anvil-pole shears is used for cutting dead and dried-out

Secateurs

Description: Secateurs or pruning shears also called hand pruners is a type of scissors designed to prune hard branches of trees and shrubs, sometimes up to two centimeters thick. Secateurs have two short handles and are operated with one hand. A spring between the handles causes the jaws to open again after closing. When not in use, the jaws may be held closed by a safety catch or by a loop holding the handles together.

Some types are designed for right-handed or left-handed use only, and some incorporate a rotating handle to reduce friction and minimize hand stress during repetitive use. There are also longer versions called telescopic pruners, which are adjustable for long-reach and operate by means of a rod system inside of a telescoping pole between the handles and the blades.

Figure 2-68: Pruning secateurs

Types of secateurs

Heavy duty secateurs: Heavy duty secateurs have sharp blades combined with unique ergonomic handles to provide an excellent secateurs range. Extra large thumb catch is positioned for natural action and maximum ease of use.

Figure 2-69: Secateurs

Uses: Secateurs or pruning shears are used in gardening, arboriculture, farming, flower arranging, and nature conservation, where fine-scale habitat management is required. Pruning secateurs are designed for clean trim & accurate hedge cut, and for soft nature grows).

Needle nose fruit secateurs

Description: Carbon steel snip needle nose fruit secateurs is made of 190mm pointed carbon steel, cuts up to 7mm diameter stems. The handles were made of aluminum alloy with hammered nickel finish. It unique centre lock, precision ground blades and comfortable rubber grips. Its overall weight is about120g

Figure 2-70: Needle nose fruit secateurs

Uses: Needle nose fruit secateurs is used as picker for fruit & flowers

Christmas tree pruning knives

Description: Brush king Christmas tree pruning knives is equipped with straight or serrated blades, made of high quality stainless steel and 41cm long. The handles are made of high strength, lightweight timber. It has overall length of 67cm and average weight of about 210g

Figure 2-71: Brush king Christmas tree pruning knives

Uses: It is used for easily pruning lower new growth

Garden knives

Description: A knife is a cutting tool with an exposed and extremely sharp, high-quality stainless steel cutting edge or blade, hand-held or otherwise, with or without a handle. Garden knife varied in design and functions some of which include:

Figure 2-72: Garden knife

Uses: They are ideal for horticultural operations such as grafting, budding, patching girdling and pruning as well as tree nurseries and handicraft.

Heavy pruning knife

Heavy pruning knife featuring a curved 76mm stainless steel blades, Hardwood handle with solid brass lining made in Switzerland. It is designed for desuckering and heavy pruning,

Figure 2-73: Heavy pruning knife (Felco 19300)

Grafting

Grafting describes any of a number of techniques in which a section of a stem with leaf buds is inserted into the stock of a tree. The upper part of the graft (the scion) becomes the top of the plant; the lower portion (the understock) becomes the root system or part of the trunk.

Grafting knives

Description: Grafting knife could be the straight type or foldable type. The folding grafting knife is designed for easy storage/carrying. It is made of 40-60mm high carbon steel forged blade with solid brass insert and brass rivet hardwood handle. Total (open) length is 160-165mm and weighs between 55-65g

Figure 2-74: Grafting knifes

Grafting knife uses: Versatile knife for florists, gardeners and tree nurseries. Required for accurate cut when grafting

Grafting knife

Typical examples of field grafting tools include

Light grafting and general pruning knife is made up of 57mm curved stainless steel blade, red nylon handle with standard alloy lining made in Switzerland

Figure 2-75: Felco 39060 grafting/pruning knife

All purpose grafting knife with bark lifter featuring a red nylon handle and separate brass bark lifter, 51mm stainless steel blade and 32mm brass bark lifter made in Switzerland

Figure 2-76: All purpose grafting knife (Felco 39110)

Field grafting pliers is designed to cut up to 14mm diameter perfect "V" shape on the scion and rootstock when placed on the anvil and the pliers. The tool is made in Italy

Figure 2-77: Grafting pliers

Scion graft crafter

Description: This is a multipurpose grafting guillotine made in New Zealand capable of being secured to bench top

Figure 2-78: Scion graft crafter

Uses: It is used in preparing high quality grafts and scion wood ideal for whip and tongue grafts without the need for training or knife skills - unskilled people can prepare, cut & assemble whip & tongue grafts safely and efficiently with minimal practice or training. It is also suitable for producing whip, V notch and chip buds

PVC grafting tapes

Description: This is a 50m length roll and 12/25mm wide translucent grafting/budding PVC or synthetic rubber tape with high elasticity, self adhesive, bio-degradable, self bursting and embossed finish ideal for binding together graft and buds. Roll could be perforated in 70mm lengths - each piece is sufficient for 1 graft.

Figure 2-79: PVC grafting tapes

Grafting wax

Description: Grafting wax is made for sealing grafts or tree wounds. It will not drip in hot weather or develop cracks in frosty weather. Typical example of grafting wax is the 454g block manufactured in Switzerland.

Figure 2-80: Grafting wax

Uses: It provides a firmly adhering, air tight and water tight covering, which can be freshly applied at any time.

Budding

Budding is a method of grafting in which the scion (upper portion of the graft) is a single bud rather than a piece of stem or twig. It is the most commonly used method for fruit tree production in the nursery, but can also be used for top working plum, cherry, apricots, and peach as well as young apple and pear trees.

Budding knife

Typical examples of budding knife include

i.   *Rose budding knife* features a black nylon handle and solid brass insert, 57mm stainless steel blade with bark lifter made in Switzerland

Figure 2-81: Rose budding knife

Budding knife uses: Budding and pruning knife suitable for plant budding and pruning

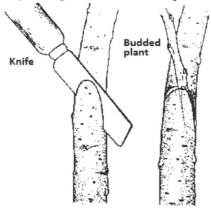

Figure 2-82: Budding knife and budded plant

ii. *The fruit tree budding knife* featuring a black nylon handle and solid brass insert, 44mm curved stainless steel blade and 13mm thumb supporter made in Switzerland

Figure 3-83: Fruit tree budding knife

iii. *Patch budding tools:* Patching is a type of budding in which there is a cut on the stock in a rectangular patch, removing the patch of bark completely. Patch budding tools include double-bladed knives and rectangular cutting blades.

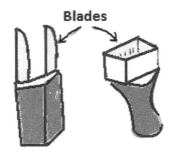

Figure 2-84: Patching knifes

Uses: Used for thick-barked trees such as walnuts, ficus, hevea (rubber tree) etc.

Tree wound sealant

Description: This is a unique blend of rubber latex and bitumen which has superior elasticity and water resistance quality, non-solvent and non-toxic. It is available in 2L or 10L containers. It can be applied with a brush or trowel direct from the container. Apply a thick, generous coat covering the entire surface of the pruning cut as soon as possible following pruning.

Figure 2-85: Tree wound sealant (Ryset)

Uses: Tree wound sealant *is* useful for tree wound dressing and sealing grafts

Tying tools

Tying tool use in horticultural works differs in design depending on manufacturers. Two examples tying tools are Sono tying tool and Ligatex tying tool.

Descriptions: The Sono tying tool made in Japan is a one-hand wire tying tool for securing vines to trellis wires etc. It twines in double operation using Ecofil paper coated wire, 200m rolls x 0.4mm diameter, then cut.

Figure 2-86: Sono tying tool

The Ligatex tying tool is another type of tying tool made in France with advanced single handed vine binding tool used in tying cordon to training wire after pruning in 3 seconds simple binding operation: push the tool, pull the tool, then lift. The binding wire spool is attached to the tool, resulting in faster, and trouble free operation. The weight of tool with new wire spool is approximately 500g

Figure 2-87: Ligatex tying tool

Girdling operation

Girdling is a gardening operation involving cutting through the cambium around the entire tree circumference. Girdling is also expressed as a means of stripping a layer of bark and the underlying cambium and phloem in a band round the trunk.

Figure 2-88: Girdling processes

It is an effective means of killing individual trees or excluding a particular tree species. With girdling, the upper part of the tree still remains alive, since photosynthesis can continue.

Eventually, however, the roots die, and the whole tree dies. The first year after girdling, the clone may appear almost normal, but by the second year the clone usually dies. For girdling to be affective the whole clone must be treated. It is also important to make the girdle in such a way that the underlying xylem is not damaged.

Girdling tools

Girdling can be performed with a chainsaw, axe, or specialized girdling tool.

Girdling with saw

If girdling with a chainsaw, for each kerf saw two parallel grooves around the tree a few inche s apart, and remove the bark between the grooves with a chisel or other implement. On 　　the trees with the thickest bark, it helps to use a small saw to cut a groove in the bark, starting from the opening made by the girdling tool and going all the rest of the way around the tree.

Figure 2-89: Girdling with saw

Girdling with axe

If girdling with an axe, chop two parallel grooves around the circumference and remove the b ark with downward strokes.

Girdling with chisel

If girdling with chisel, *make a* vertical slice cut with the truck spring blade, deep enough to get to the part of the bark that needs separation. stick the chisel into the split between the outer and inner layers. push the chisel hard to split the bark and tear it away from the trunk. Move around the tree, tearing and pushing the bark. The break in the bark only needs to be a few inches wide, but usually the bark tears farther than that, and makes a girdle at least 6 or 8 inches wide. pry the bark, as it splits along the sawed line.

Figure 2-90: Stripping off the bark

Girdling with specialized tools

Specialized girdling knives (Figure 2-83) cut and removes strips of bark tissue from the trunk or branch of vines and fruit trees. Some of its features include high quality stainless steel blade with timber handle and bark scraper available in 2mm, 3mm, 4.8mm or 6mm sizes.

Figure 2-91: Girdling/ring barking knives

Girdling with scorp

Another tool that works well for girdling is a "scorp" a wood carver's tool for hollowing out wooden bowls

Figure 2-92: Scorp knifes

Tapener gun

This is a high speed single handed tape gun made in Japan for dispensing, stapling and cutting tape ideal for staking plants, training vines and fruit trees. By simply squeezing the handle, the tape gun wraps tape around the stem, then cuts the tape and staples it securely in one action. It can use 15μm (standard) and 25μm (heavy duty) thickness tapes.

Max tapener

Sono tapener

Figure 2-93: Tapener guns

2.2.5 Harvest and picking tools and description

Picking and trimming snip

Description: Picking and trimming snips made from stainless steel blades, soft spring and ergonomic handles, overall length of 185mm and weighs 110g

Figure 2-94: Picking and trimming snip

Uses: Picking and trimming snips are suitable for grape harvesting, flower and fruit picking and light trimming

Picking shears

Description: Picking shears made is from stainless steel blades, soft spring and ergonomic handles, overall length of 200mm and weighs 120g

Figure 2-95: Picking shears

Uses: Picking and trimming shears is suitable for grape harvesting, flower and fruit picking and light trimming

By-pass stainless shear

Description: By-pass stainless shears are either curved, pointed or blunt nosed tips made from 15cm stainless steel, ergonomic palm contour fit handle with thumb/finger ring, soft rubber cover steel handles and centre slide lock. It has light weight and strong durable construction

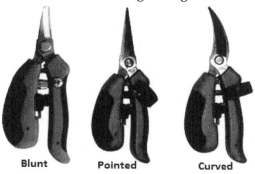

Blunt   Pointed   Curved

Figure 2-96: By-pass stainless shears

Uses: By-pass stainless shear is suitable for fruit & flower harvest and picking

Grape harvest scissors

Description: Grape harvest scissors are designed either as straight or curved head and has an overall length of 150mm, 40mm blade length made of stainless steel alloy for long life, resists corrosion and holds edge, ergonomic soft handles to provide less fatigue with extended use, 0.05mm blade serration for tough jobs, and weighs 52g

Figure 2-97: Horticultural/craft scissors

Uses: Grape harvest scissors with straight or curved head are used for picking grape and other horticultural crops

Secateurs

Majority of fruits and vegetables are harvested by hands using secateurs, clippers, knives or diggers. Some fruits such as citrus, grapes and mangoes, need to be clipped or cut from the plant (Figure).

Figure 2-98: Harvesting with secateurs

Sickles

Sickles are hand held agricultural tools with varying designs of blades used for harvesting grain crops or cutting succulent forage chiefly for feeding livestock (either freshly cut or dried as hay). They can be short handled or long handled depending on the type of operation. The blade edges could be single, double, straight or serrated edge.

Figure 2-99: Sickle

Common examples of short handled sickles include

- *Mini sickle:* The mini sickle with 180mm replaceable blades is available in single and double edge blade versions. They come in 3 blade positions: 95 deg sickle style, 140 degree or in-line with the handle taper ground, razor sharp carbon steel blade. Each weighs approximately 275g

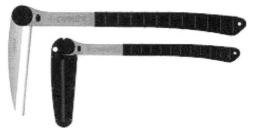

Figure 2-100: Mini sickles

Uses: Useful for cutting through grass tufts, light vines or weeds

- *Narrow serrated sickle:* Serrated sickle come in two sizes; narrow and large sizes. The narrow serrated sickle is equipped with 115mm stainless steel blade, has a plastic handle and the blade is serrated (photo shows non-serrated). It has an overall length of 260mm and weighs 70g

Figure 2-101: Narrow serrated sickle (Barnel BLK720)

Uses: It is ideal for tropical fruits, bananas, vegetables, flowers harvesting etc

- *Large serrated sickle:* Large serrated sickle features a 155mm stainless steel blade, plastic handle (not timber) and an overall length of 340mm, weighing 100g.

Figure 2-102: Large serrated sickle (Barnel BLK727)

- *Long handle sickle:* Long handle sickle is equipped long wooden handle with 205mm stainless steel non-serrated blade and 610mm overall length weighing 290g

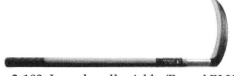

Figure 2-103: Long handle sickle (Barnel BLK737)

Uses: Ideal for fruit & vegetable harvesting on tall trees etc

Harvest/landscape shears

Description: Harvest / landscape shears *are* precision tools with high carbon steel Teflon coated blades for smooth cuts, Strong stainless steel handle construction equipped with cushioned TPR grips and leather pouch

Figure 2-104: Harvest/landscape shears (Barnel B3333)

Fruit picker

Description: Fruit picker is equipped with straight or curved blades, made of high quality stainless steel. Its handles were made of soft PVC grips designed for comfort and has light weight (120g)

Figure 2-105: Fruit pickers

Uses: Fruit picker is designed for avocado, flower and fruit picking.

Picking bag

Fresh fruits harvested by hand were dropped into suitable picking bags hung on shoulders to avoid damage. Cloth bag with openings on both ends can be easily worn over the shoulders with an adjustable harness (Figure 2-106). In case metallic buckets are to be used for harvesting, fitting cloth over the opened bottom can reduce damage to crop. Fitting canvas bags with adjustable harnesses or by simply adding some carrying straps to baskets also helps to reduce handling losses.

Figure 2-106: Picking bags

Steel reinforced picking bag

Description: Steel reinforced harvest picking bag is equipped with a steel reinforced open mouth design for fast picking, the front lip is padded & vinyl reinforced to protect the fruit a wide over-the-shoulder padded straps, fully adjustable for comfort and fit. The bag allows a full range of motion whether working from a ladder, climbing a tree or on the ground.

Figure 2-107: Harvest picking bag on display

Harvest picking bag is worn in front of the body, having the over-the-shoulder padded straps secured in place for effective carriage. Easily adjust load and weight with rope ties which unhook to empty fruit safely through the bottom.

Figure 2-108: Harvest picking bag

Picking bucket

Description: Picking buckets such as cherry picking buckets are rectangular plastic bucket of size 35cm (l) x 25cm (w) x 20cm (d) equipped with adjustable double straps lumbar harness. The internal volume is approximately 12 ltrs and weighs 750g with harness.

Figure 2-109: Cherry picking buckets

Uses: Picking buckets are suitably used for picking fruits such as cherries, olives etc.

Premium cherry picking bucket

Description: Premium cherry picking bucket is extra heavy duty kidney shaped fruit picking bucket equipped with adjustable double straps lumbar harness, size 44cm(l) x 30cm(w) x 20cm(d) and internal volume capacity approximately 18 ltrs and weighs 1.5kg with harness

Figure 2-110: premium cherry picking buckets

Uses: Picking buckets are suitably used for picking fruits such as cherries, olives etc.

Fruit picking bag

Description: Fruit picking bags are extremely lightweight and comfortable bags having a hardened steel frame around the top and bottom supported by 25mm thick foam lined with tough waterproof polyester material. It has extra deep fully lined exit chutes secured by rope and hardened steel hook. It is equipped with lumbar harness with adjustable straps. Typical examples of fruit picking bag include:

- The Coppo bag manufactured in New Zealand with size 54cm (l) x 30cm (w) x 23cm(d), an approximate 0.6 Bushel Capacity weighing 2.1kg and

Figure 2-111: Coppo fruit picking bags

- Canvas fruit picking bags made in Australia include heavy duty 18oz cotton canvas equipped with padded cross-over shoulder straps, long exit chute with hardened steel clips, plastic reinforced hoop and walls available in 0.5 case, 1 case and 1.5 case capacities

Figure 2-112: Canvas fruit picking bags

Uses: Fruit picking bags are suitable for fruit picking such as apples or other precious fruit

Collection sacks

Description: The collection bags can be hand woven from strong cord or sewn from canvas. The hoop used as the collection bag rim and sharp cutting edges can be made from sheet metal, steel tubing or recycled scrap metal.

Tripod ladders

Description: A ladder with three legs is very convenient and more stable than a common ladder (Figure 2-105). A ladder helps harvesting crops such as mango, pears, peaches, plums without damaging tree branches.

Figure 2-113: Tripod ladder

Picking poles

Description: These tools can be easily made by hand. A long pole attached to a collection bag, allow the harvester to cut catch produce growing on a tree without climbing on tree.

Figure 2-114: Picking pole

Tele poles

Description: Professional fruit picking telescopic and fiberglass pole sections is equipped with a quick release mechanism which provides rapid change of heads (lopper/claw/fruit picker) on telescopic poles. The handle is equipped with a safety lock and pole that extends to 6-feet or 9-feet allowing easy reach and fruit pick. In operation, just hold the fruit and twist the harvester making picking fruit easy without having to get on the ladder.

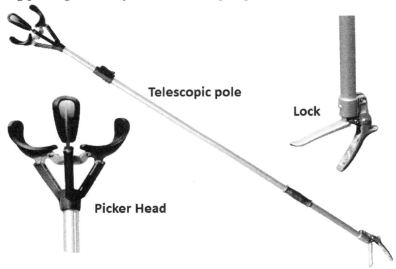

Figure 2-115: Tele poles for fruit picking

Fruit picking heads

Fruit picker head is optimally designed with a broad opening which directs the fruit to the end of the tips for easy pulling from the branch. The fruit picking heads varies in design depending on manufacturers. Three different designs are common: the lopper, claw and bag picker heads. The picker heads are equipped with cotton bags for fruit collection, which can be removed for washing.

Types of *fruit picking heads*

- *Claw picker head:* The claw head fruit picker has three "bruise free" soft rubber padded claws to keep each piece of fruit safe from damage.

Figure 2-116: Fruit picking head

- *Lopper picker head:* A tree lopper picker head is a manually operated hand tool with long telescopic bypass handles for pruning of orchard trees in standing position. The shape of the lopping shear is similar to pruning secateurs or hedge shear depending upon the manufacturers. The shear consists of two shearing blades joined to the sockets to which wooden handles are inserted. The blades are fabricated from high carbon steel, tool steel or alloy steel, forged to shape and the cutting edges are hardened to 425-450 HB.

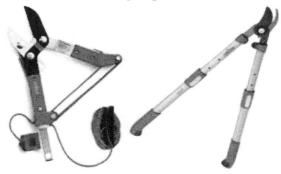

Figure 2-117: Tree lopper (left) telescopic bypass lopper (right) heads

Uses: It is used for pruning and cutting of the twigs, which are beyond the reach of human hands and cannot be cut with pruning secateurs

- *Bag picker head:* Bag picker heads are essentially used for similar purposes of picking and storing fruits, however, they differ in design and material of production. When it is harvest time, this neatly designed head pulls the fruit neatly from the branch with no damage.

A few designs of bag picker heads were presented below.

  - *See-through fruit bag:* The bag fruit picker head has a large capacity see-through fruit bag. In operation, a razor sharp "U" shaped bypass fruit picking cutter will cut up to 7mm fruit stems and includes 6.3m pull rope. There is replaceable bag and an adjustable cutter angle which enables easy access into tight spots. The picking head weighs 800g

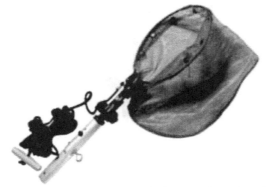

Figure 2-118: See-through fruit picking head

o *Fiber bag*: Fiber bag design has a lightweight design for added durability. The picker head can be used with regular or telescopic shafts

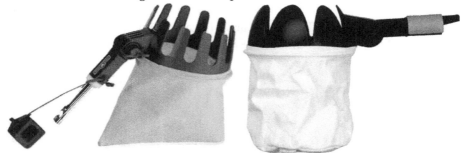

Figure 2-119: Fiber bag fruit picking heads

o *Aesthetic designs:* Other designs include some special aesthetic design features such as shapes, aperture adjuster etc. for acceptability and promotion. Some are shown below.

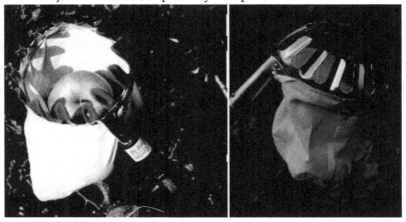

Figure 2-120: Aesthetic fruit picking heads

2.2.6 Products transport cart and description

Lifting horticultural inputs around the garden can really be burdensome without carrying aids such as wheelbarrows or carts. Garden wheelbarrows and carts are indispensable garden tools. Distribution of plants, soil and compost around the garden may be cumbersome without the help of such aids. The size of your cart will depend on the size of your garden.

Wheel barrows

Description: These wheel barrows are in customized sizes and dimensions according to farm requirement. Some attributes desirable of an ergonomic wheelbarrow are: a stale stance, handles that extend all the way to the tyre, an air filled tyre (with tube) and a deep tray with a reinforced undercarriage.

Figure 2-121: Wheel barrows

Some of the basic features required of wheel barrow include:

- Easy to be cleaning
- Light weight
- Durability
- Availability in single wheel & double wheel

Uses: Wheel barrows are widely used in various gardening operations for handling smaller size particles gathering and conveyance such as fruit and vegetable handling, manure handling etc.

Canvas cart

Description: These are one wheeled hand pushed garden carts with deep canvas container/tray and two rubber grip handles for comfort when in use. They are characterized by light weight and ease of cleaning.

Uses: Canvas cart is widely used in collection and distribution of fruits and vegetables as well as handling smaller size particles gathering

Figure 2-122: Canvas cart

Drawn carts

Two types of drawn carts are common; drawn 2-wheeled steel carts and drawn 4-wheeled utility garden steel carts

- *Drawn 2-wheeled steel carts:* Two-wheeled garden carts can be powered manually or tractor drawn. Two-wheeled garden carts are becoming more and more popular because the two wheels makes for a more stable ride with heavy loads. To have a smooth and stable ride it is advisable to source for large, spoke wheels. Deep buckets are good for dumping. Flat beds are preferable for shoveling out of the cart.

Figure 2-123: 2-wheel drawn steel cart

Uses: Hand drawn carts are used for field packing. Harvesters place an empty carton on the cart, then pick, sort, grade and pack directly into the container. Filled cartons are moved immediately into coolers or keep in a well-shaded area.

- *Drawn 4-wheeled utility garden steel carts:* This is a traditional, flat bed gardening cart capable of hauling up to 880 lbs weight. It also has the versatility to carry extra wide loads when the sides are dropped down. They are often equipped with dual pulling system for pulling by hand (handle in front) or tractor tow bracket behind. The frame is made from powder-coated steel material while the handle is straight with foam rubber grip for comfort. Also included is a removable nylon liner for easy cleaning and emptying.

Figure 2-124: 4-wheel drawn steel cart

The mesh sides of the cart can be folded down or removed to convert into a flat bed cart. The all-terrain Pneumatic wheels helps in cart manoeuvring wherever you go and allow it to handle tough terrain and four undercarriage cross beams provide overall cargo support. The iinside dimensions of the containment area are not limited to specific dimension but varies from; 38" long 20" wide 10" high to 48" long x 24" wide x 26.77" high

Figure 2-125: 4-wheel drawn steel cart

Uses: The wagon is used when working in the yard or garden to haul plants, pine straw, sticks, rocks or any other lawn, farm or gardening supplies up to 600 pounds.

Lawn carts

Description: This is horticultural equipment consisting of a container body made from an 18 gauge metal plate or durable lightweight plastic and mounted on a heavy steel undercarriage frame with a removable tailgate over the wheels for the purposes of dumping.

Figure 2-126: Lawn cart (plastic body)

The removable tailgate gives easy access to the cart bed. The body size varies according to designed capacity. The most popular ones measures 30"W x 48"L x 12"H with a carrying capacity of 10 cu. ft. and 1000 lbs weight capacity. The wheels have oil lube bearings, grease fittings for easy lubrication and longer life. The 4.00 x 8 tires are well suited for use over uneven terrain.

Figure 2-127: Lawn cart (metal body)

Push/pull lawn roller

Description: This is horticultural equipment consisting of a roller, a steel handle for manual use or draw bar for use with any lawn tractor, and a scraper bar/ blade for self cleaning.

Figure 2-128: Push/pull roller (manual)

The roller is built empty with 14 gauge metals with varying sizes from 18″ to 24″ width and 24" diameter for manual use. The roller in use may be filled with sand or water to a capacity of 6.05 cu.ft for manual drawn rollers and 15.32 cu.ft. for tractor

Uses: Push/pull lawn rollers are used for maintaining smooth existing lawn or setting new seed beds.

2.3   Hand held power tools, description and uses

A wide range of hand held power tools, including hand cultivators, electric hedge trimmers, lawn aerators, leaf sweepers and leaf blowers, have been popular among hand held tools employed in gardening operations. A range of such tools are described below with their utilization.

Hedge trimmer

Description: Hedge trimmers are designed as lightweight and powerful tools with a cutter bar having two sets of reciprocating blades. The teeth along the top blade are diamond round and double edged for durability. The cutter bar is driven either by engine or an induction motor. A baffle guard is provided to protect the user from flying leaves, stems or branches. The motor power unit is provided with flexible chord, which permits the movement of the trimmer to all places in the garden. An extra trigger switch is integrated in the handle for quick, error free operation.

Figure 2-129: Hedge trimmer (Bosch AHS50-16)

Other features such as effortless handling due to its lightweight, dynamically balanced, and ergonomic handle are added advantage. Electric hedge trimmers are powered by a 450 watt high power induction motor, and a blade length of 50cm, with a blade spacing of 16mm ideal for cutting younger- small - medium sized hedges.

Uses: Electric hedge trimmers are used for trimming hedges, shrubs and brambles. It is also used for contouring plants in desired shapes and sizes for enhancing the aesthetics of the garden.

Leaf blower

Description: Leaf blower *is* an engine-driven gardening device used to generate forced air out of a nozzle for the purposes of debris removal. Some units can also suck in leaves and small twigs via a vacuum, and shred them into a bag. In that role it is called a blower vac.

Figure 2-130: Leaf blower

Leaf blowers are usually powered by two-stroke engine or an electric motor, but four-stroke engines were recently introduced to partially address air pollution concerns. Leaf blowers are typically self-contained handheld units, or backpack mounted units with a handheld wand. The latter is more ergonomic for prolonged use.

Figure 2-131: Backpack leaf blower

Uses: Leaf blower is used to remove yard wastes, fallen leaves and other debris.

Leaf sweeper

Description: This is lightweight battery powered equipment comprising of a blow tube with built-in scraper, a soft grip handle and a power command speed control system designed for easy clearing of debris from hard surfaces. A36-Volt lithium ion battery provides longer runtime and longer battery life year after year. The innovative power command system controls speed for maximum run-time or maximum power.

Figure 2-132: Leaf sweeper

An innovative leaf sweeper design has features such as LSW36 cordless sweeper, LBX36 36-Volt lithium-ion battery, blow tube and LCS36 36-Volt fast charger capable of recharging a 36-Volt battery in about 1 hour.

Uses- Leaf sweeper is ideal for blowing driveways, sidewalks, decks, garages and other hard surfaces of leaves, grass clippings, and other lawn debris.

Push leaf sweeper

Uses: Collect a huge amount of leaves from lawns or paths by simply pushing the sweeper along

Description: Push leaf sweeper is equipped with a 24" clearing width, height adjustable device, 10" diameter wheels and lightweight and similar in operation to hand sweeper

Flame guns

Description: The flame gun consists of a one gallon tank, integral pressure pump, pressure gauge, precision control valve and a burner. The flame gun operates at 2000 degrees Fahrenheit which destroys weeds, spores and bacteria organically with no poison hazards for crops, soil, pets or wildlife.

Figure 2-133: Flame guns (Sheen X300)

Uses: The flame gun is perfect for all weed killing operations, cultivation of cleared soil and rough ground clearance.

Power saw

Description: Power chain saw is a light and portable machine normally operated by one person. Cutting is done by an endless chain fitted with cutters, which runs around a flat piece called the bar. The drive link of the chain runs in a groove machined in the edge of the bar and is pulled along by the teeth of a sprocket, which engage them.

Figure 2-134: Power saw

The sprocket in turn is driven at full speed either by small two- stroke petrol engine or electric motor. The power to the chain is transmitted through a centrifugal clutch mounted on crankshaft of the engine. The chain is of roller type and has left and right hand cutters spaced alternately along its length. In front of each of the cutters is a small projection called a depth gauge whose purpose is to control the depth of cut made by the cutter.

Uses: The chain saw is a time saving and efficient power tool used in tree felling and horticultural operations and are more effective than axe or machete in large size vegetations.

Brush cutter

Description: Brush cutter is an implement (either hand held or tractor-mounted) for clearing brush and small trees from areas when preparing land for agricultural crops, clearing routes for the construction of roads and canals, and setting up forest cuttings. The head contains a safety shield on the user side and a rotating hub which may also be called a head or spool.

Figure 2-135: Hand held BC520F brush cutter

There are three types of hand held brush cutters:

a. Ones that use two horizontal blades secured to a frame at an angle of about 60° to each other;
b. Ones that cut the wood into chunks and press it into the ground with a roller that has blades fixed to its surface and
c. Ones that use horizontal blades revolving on a vertical axis.

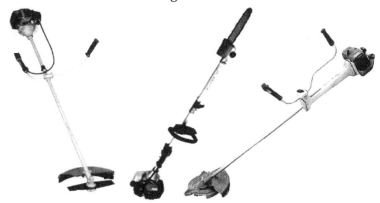

Figure 2-136: Hand held brush cutters

Back strapped brush cutters

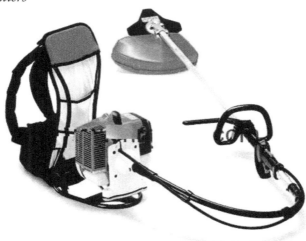

Figure 2-137: Back strap brush cutter BC520F

String trimmer

Description: A string trimmer, also called a "weed eater" or a "weed-wacker", is a powered handheld device that uses a flexible mono-filament line instead of a blade for cutting grass and other plants near objects. It consists of a cutting head at the end of a long shaft with a handle or handles and sometimes a shoulder strap.

Figure 2-138: String trimmers cutting head

Operation mechanism: A string trimmer, also known as a "weed whip", works on the principle that a line that is turned fast enough is held out from its housing (the rotating reel) very stiffly by the string tension that exerts the centripetal force that prevents the string from flying off in a straight line under its own inertia. The faster it turns the stiffer the line. The operator controls the height at which cutting take place and can trim down to ground level quite easily. As the line is worn, or breaks off, the operator knocks the reel on the ground so that a release mechanism allows some of the line in the reel to extend and replace the spent portion.

Figure 2-138: String trimmer in action

The newer models have an 'auto-feed' operation where a small cutter on the line-guard ensures that the line length exposed for cutting does not exceed the length that can be swung efficiently by the motor. Newly extended line operates more efficiently because of its heavier weight and surface effects. The speed of the spinning hub is usually controlled by a trigger on the handle.

For vertical cutting the whole machine can be tilted or some trimmers allow the head to be adjusted at different angles. Vertical cutting is not recommended near sidewalks or other concrete and pavement edges, because it leaves open grooves that allow water to collect and cause damage.

Large trimmers, used for cutting roadside grass in large areas, are often heavy enough to require two hands to operate, and some are even fitted with a harness enabling the user's strength to bear some of its weight. These very large trimmers are often referred to as brush cutters.

Trimmers that have nylon or metal blades usually require straight drive shafts to handle the higher torque required to turn the heavier disk, and because of the shock loads that are passed back from the blade to the drive shaft and its gearbox(es). Smaller line trimmers have curved drive shafts to make holding the cutting-head at ground level much easier and with less strain on the operator.

Types of string trimmer

String trimmers powered by an internal combustion engine have the engine on the opposite end of the shaft from the cutting head while electric string trimmers typically have an electric motor in the cutting head, but some other arrangements exist too. One of such is an arrangement where the trimmer is connected to heavy machinery and is powered using a hydraulic motor.

Disadvantages of engine-powered string trimmer

Disadvantages of a gasoline-powered string trimmer include its greater weight and the significant vibration that carries throughout the device, both of which interfere with its maneuverability and contribute to muscle fatigue, as well as the requirement that motor oil be added to its fuel (if it is equipped with a two-stroke engine).

Advantages of engine-powered string trimmer

Advantages of gasoline-powered trimmers include mobility (because they are not attached to a power outlet) and the higher maximum power.

Accessories

Many string trimmers allow the hub, the head or the lower part of the shaft to be replaced with accessories. Common accessories include:

- Replacing the monofilament line with metal or plastic blades.
- Replacing the lower shaft with a small chain saw to create a powered pole saw.
- Replacing the lower shaft with a hedge trimmer.
- Replacing the lower shaft with a cultivator.

Quick release shafts are offered on many newer models which do not require any tools to switch in accessories. Typically only gasoline powered trimmers offer shaft powered accessories, as electric or battery driven units don't generate enough power.

2.4   Guidelines for selection gardening tools

The right tool makes any job easier and that is no exception in the garden. Gardeners collect many tools over the years, but there is always one tool that they absolutely couldn't garden without. If you are just starting out, there are a few basic tools that will get you started.

Well maintained tools matched to the person and the task, used infrequently at well-designed workstations does not cause harm. It is when they do not match the person or the task or are used repeatedly and/or for long periods that hand tool and work area design become critical.

The best garden tool to select is one that:

1. Matches the task you are doing
2. Fits the workspace available
3. Reduces the force that needed to be applied
4. Fits your hand
5. Can be used in a comfortable position
6. Is well maintained.

Fit the tool to the worker, not the worker to the tool

When tools require force, handle size should allow the worker to grip all the way around the handle so that the forefinger and thumb overlap by 3/8".

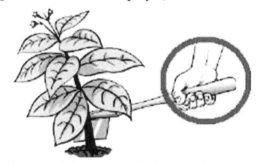

Figure 2-139: Handle diameter is large enough for small overlap of thumb and fingers

Handle diameter should range from 1-3/8" for small hands to 2-1/8" for large hands, with an average of 1-3/4". Handles should be covered with smooth, slip-resistant material (plastic or rubber). Dual-handled tools (like shears or pliers) should have a handle length of at least 4"and preferably 5". They should have a spring return to maintain an open position, and handles that are almost straight without finger grooves.

Figure 2-140: Bad ergonomic tool

Poorly designed tool handle: Handle presses into base of palm and no spring release device to return the handle. It requires user to open after each cut.

Figure 2-141: Good ergonomic tool

Well-designed tool: Handles are long. Spring return keeps tool open. Handles are covered with rubber or plastic grip.

CHAPTER 3

GARNENING PRACTICE & OPERATION

Content: Selection of gardening site, site planning, bed preparation, planting, post planting activities, harvesting and handling

3   Introduction

Vegetables are mainly grown for 2 reasons: for home consumption: they add minerals and vitamins to the diet and improve the health of the farmer family and for the market to earn money by supplying surplus vegetables for sale in the market at a good price. Depending on the market situation, you have to decide which vegetables to grow. If you live in a rural area, the traditional vegetables will have a better market. If you live near a town, the production of "modern" vegetables can be profitable.

Selecting a site

The choice of site is dependent on edaphic factors such as soil and other social factors. Vegetable garden should be situated as near as possible:

1. *To the house*: Proximity to the house is of essence you want to harvest a lot of vegetables of good quality. This will allow enough time to look after them very well.
2. *To a water source*: Vegetables need a lot of water to grow well; as such locating them far from water source implies a lot of work to carry the water.

Protection

Vegetable garden should be well protected against

a. Destruction by animals, pilfering, etc.
b. Exposure to excessive wind, sun and rain

c. Water logging; choose a level place with loose, well drained and fertile soil.

Selection of size of gardening plot

The size of a gardening (e. g. vegetable) plot should be about 9 or 10 square meters (3m x 3m, 2.5m x 3.5m or 1m x 10m). A square plot is best but if it may not be practicable because of irregular shape of land, you could use a rectangular plot instead. However there is no restriction to the size of your plot. The two plots shown in Figure below cover roughly the same area of ground.

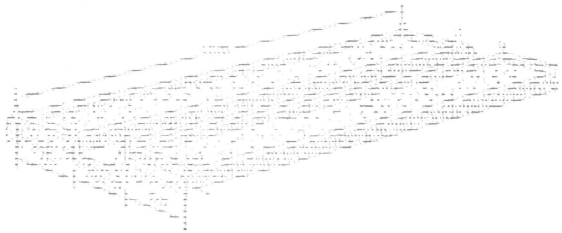

Figure 3-1: Vegetable plot size

The best direction (aspect)

Conventionally, one side of your plot should face the north. One way to find the direction of the north is to point your *right arm* towards where the *sun rises* and your *left arm* towards where the *sun sets*. Then you are facing north. Draw the symbol, N, facing up the page to show the direction of north.

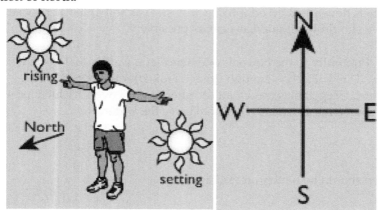

Figure 3-2: Vegetable plot size

Relative position of plot from prevailing wind

Shelter your farm plot from the prevailing wind. Ideally your vegetable plot should be protected from wind. It is not always possible to have a good aspect with plenty of sun and protection from wind at the same time. Sheltering field from the wind, if not carefully done, could end up shading an area too much for good plant growth to occur.

An arrow on a plan shows the most common direction the wind comes from and represents the main wind direction or prevailing wind. The site plan below shows the main wind direction and the direction of north for a section.

3.2   Site plan selection and preparation

Site plan is a layout drawing showing the main growing areas where the owners wish to grow a particular plant. In this case the areas include: vegetable garden, lawn, shrubs, flowerbeds, trees, clothesline etc.

You may find out that you can fit your plot into an existing vegetable garden. If not, you'll need to find a convenient space. You may need to use a waste area or part of a lawn or flowerbed.

Preparation of your garden (tillage)

Now it's time to get on with the hard work and prepare your garden plot for sowing seeds. Digging is important because it breaks up soil into smaller pieces. This is called *cultivation*. The condition of the soil is called *tilth*. When the soil feels all fine and crumbly it is called a fine tilth.

The main reasons for soil preparation or conditioning are to:

1   Improve drainage
2   Let air into the soil (*aeration*)
3   Encourage roots to grow deeply
4   Control weeds.

Steps to cultivate your garden

Mark out your plot: Measure out your plot 3 m x 3 m or whatever size is possible. Peg each corner of the plot marked out. For instance, the diagram shows a square plot.

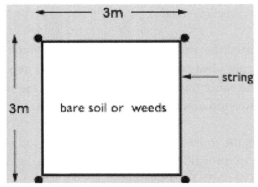

Figure 3-3: Pegging plot size

To help you remember which side is the north side, mark the two corner pegs on the north side. You can use something like paint, wool or string.

Figure 3-4: Removing weed

Remove the weeds

If any weed I needed to be removed, try to remove the whole plant including the roots using a hand fork, spade or trowel to loosen weeds, and then pull the whole plant out by hand.

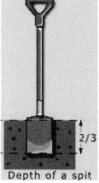

Figure 3-5: Depth of digging

Planning for garden bed

Selection of the type of gardening practice between conventional vegetable garden and organic gardening is essential. The conventional vegetable garden with row cropping, takes up too much space and isn't that productive as gardening beds, however, organic garden beds are more productive, because they conserve space, water, and fertilizers inputs. The size of plot in gardening is equally a factor in planning your garden. We need to conserve space and at the same time, make the space to be more productive than conventional vegetable gardening.

Advantages of vegetable garden beds

- Deep soil preparation requirement in vegetable garden beds creates great soil structure. On established mature beds, shallow cultivation can be used for several years until compaction requires deep soil preparation.
- Fertilizing garden beds using organic fertilizers and compost is a significant factor of soil fertility and soil organic matter.
- Vegetable garden beds gives room for close plant spacing practice as it is in nature.
- Vegetable garden beds promotes the growth of carbon-efficient crops on 60% of the growing area in a year for grain (calories) and large amounts of organic matter for composting.
- Crop production in vegetable garden beds can be 4 or more times higher than conventional agriculture.
- Dependence on outside sources of fertilizers is reduced because of the heavy use of compost and cover crops.
- Less water usage can be significantly less than conventional vegetable rows, because of close planting spacing (shades the soil) and improved soil structure.

Disadvantages of conventional vegetable gardening

- Vegetables raised in rows are subject to fluctuating temperatures, because of the high and low moisture content and the sides of the rows are exposed to the extremes of air and sun.
- A row crop garden takes up to four times the space as gardening beds.
- The wide spacing between the rows encourages more weeds.
- Soil cultivation is shallow placing the plants in a stressful state.
- Harvesting (standing between rows) and machines compacts the soil, making it difficult for plant and root growth.
- Irrigation floods the soil, drowns the roots, and washes soil from the rows and upper root zone.

Digging plot

Digging is when you turn over and mix up the topsoil. You don't need to dig too deeply. Two-thirds of a spade depth will be fine. As you dig over your plot, break down soil lumps into smaller pieces by hitting them with the spade. Rake your plot to a fine tilth

Figure 3-6: Raking to fine tilth

3.3   Planting operation and fertilizer application

Planning for planting operation

The main reason for planning your garden is to allow the plants get maximum light and space. In planning your planting, the followings are required:

Plan for the direction of the row: Rows should run north to south wherever possible. This will give the plants the most sunlight during the day because the sun rises in the east, travels in an arc and then sets in the west.

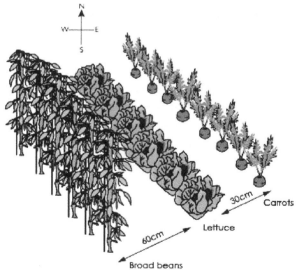

Figure 3-7: Row direction and order

Plan for the row order – which plants go in which rows? The order of the rows is important because you don't want the taller plants to shade the shorter ones. Smaller vegetables such as lettuce and carrots can be grown on the sunniest side or east side. The diagram shows the row order from tallest to shortest for broad beans, lettuce and carrots.

Plan for row spacing – how far apart the rows should be. Plants need space to grow and spread out. If plants are grown to close together they will compete with each other for light, nutrients, water and space. The taller plants, like climbing or staked plants, should be on the west side. This will prevent smaller plants from being shaded.

Remember that fully-grown plants will take up a lot more space than seeds or seedlings.

Figure 3-8: Fully grown carrots

Directions for row and plant spacing can be found on seed packets or in gardening books.

Plant grouping

Wherever possible, grow similar crops together. They will have similar growing requirements. leaf crops like spinach, and cabbage are put together because they need nitrogen fertilizer and lime. Radish and carrots will grow together in a soil that is level and with a fine tilth. Growing plants together with similar requirements will make it easy to:

- Water
- Weed
- Control pests and diseases
- Fertilize
- Harvest

Sowing seeds in a container

Seeds sown outside are usually sown in the soil, a natural growing medium. When seeds are sown in containers usually an *artificial growing media* is used. Seed raising mix is one example of an artificial growing medium. Seed raising mixes don't require many nutrients, as the seedlings are pricked out and transplanted into soil or another growing medium when they are still young.

A good growing media of any kind provides:

- Drainage
- Air around plant roots
- Enough water for plants to use
- Nutrients
- Support for the plant in the soil.

Advantages of sowing seeds in a container

Seeds sown in a container can be kept in a protected environment that provides their basic needs of warm temperatures, water and oxygen. This should increase the rate of germination.

Disadvantages of sowing seeds in a container

- Once the seeds grow, the seedlings need to be 'hardened off' to get used to harsher outdoor conditions, before they are transplanted outside in the garden or another container.
- 'Transplant shock' can slow growth or may stop it altogether for a short time.
- The seedlings will take more time for the plants to reach maturity.
- Container sowing costs more than sowing seeds directly outside.
- Some seedlings cannot be effectively transplanted, for example carrots and parsnips.

Choosing containers

Seeds can be sown in all sorts of different containers. Containers should:

- have plenty of room for roots
- have drainage holes in the bottom
- be lightweight for easy handling

Successive sowing

When a small amount of seed is sown at regular intervals over several weeks this is known as successive sowing. The crop is then harvested over a longer period of time. Successive sowing is important for home gardeners who need a steady supply of produce for eating. Crops that often have successive sowings include leafy vegetables such as cabbage and quick maturing root vegetables such as radishes.

Sowing other types of seed

- Very fine seed is spread on the surface of the media and just firmed down, not covered. You can mix the seeds with a little bit of fine dry sand then place the mixture in a pepper pot. The seeds are then sown using the pepper pot for even distribution over the surface of the media.
- Large seeds are planted individually into holes made in the media.

3.4   Caring for seedlings

Fertilizer application

Fertilizer contains nutrients that plants need for healthy growth. A plot your size will need about 1.5 kg of general fertilizer. That's about six large cupfuls. If you have general fertilizer spread this evenly over your plot.

Pricking out your seedlings

Pricking out is the term used when seedlings are needed to be transplanted from where they were first sown into another container where they will have more room. Seedlings are pricked out once they are large enough to handle. Usually this is when the seedling has four leaves, two true leaves and the first seed leaves (cotyledons).

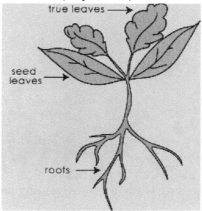

Figure 3-9: Seedling

For instance, once lettuce seedlings are at this stage, pricking out is necessary because crowded seedlings compete with each other for: Light, water, nutrients, air and space. Pricked out seedlings are graded for size. Seedlings at the same stage of development can be grown together. The Figure below show spinach seedlings that have just been pricked out; each seedling has two seed leaves and two true leaves.

Figure 3-10: Recently pricked spinach seedlings

3.5   Seedling transplant

Once your seedlings have developed a good root system and have at least two to four true leaves they can be gently transplanted into your vegetable plot. However before they are transplanted, the seedlings should be hardened off. Seedlings which are to be planted outside should be gradually hardened off to help prevent transplanting shock and any slowing of plant growth. *Hardening off* means the seedlings gradually get used to the conditions they will experience once they are transplanted.

Figure 3-11: Lettuce seedling ready for transplanting beside a lettuce seedling

To harden them off, expose the seedlings gradually to the same environmental conditions they will have in their final planting position. They will need gradual exposure until they are in the final conditions for 24 hours.

Seedlings could be placed in a cold frame that is left open for more hours each day or they could have a protective cover on them for part of the day and at night. This cover is gradually removed altogether. After 5–7 days of hardening off, the seedlings will be ready to be transplanted to their final growing position.

Transplanting technique

Transplant in the evening or on a cloudy day so that the plants are not immediately exposed to hot sun. The best way to transplant seedlings is to:

- Thoroughly water the nursery bed, so that you can lift the seedlings more easily
- Be very careful not to break the roots of the seedlings
- Choose only those seedlings that have grown well
- Prepare the seedlings by trimming off some roots and leaves. If the roots are not well trimmed, they will dry pu.

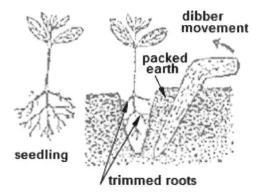

Figure 3-12: Manual transplanting of seedlings

- Transplant into well prepared holes. Pad the earth down well around the plant. If the earth is not closely placed around the roots, they will dry out.

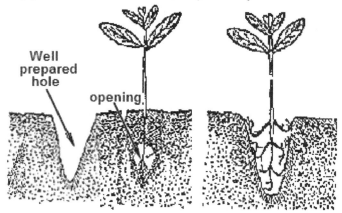

Figure 3-13: Seedlings must be transplanted correctly

- Water the transplanted seedling thoroughly. When a seedling is planted in a new growing position it experiences transplant shock.

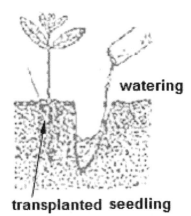

watering

transplanted seedling

Figure 3-14: Watering transplanted seedling

This can be reduced by:

- Hardening off seedlings gradually
- Watering the plants before and after transplanting
- Handling the plants gently
- Keeping as much medium as possible around the plant roots
- Holding the plants by the leaves so the tender stem is not crushed.

Mulching

In the dry season, mulching is a very important practice in both the nursery and the vegetable beds, because it helps preserve moisture in the soil, add nutrients when the mulch decays and prevent the soil from getting too hot.

Figure 3-15: Chopped grass useful as mulch

It is important to reduce the mulch level in the nursery as soon as the seedlings appear. Do not allow the mulch to touch the stem of your plants to reduce pest attach. Do not use grass that has flowered to avoid weed infestation.

Watering

Vegetables need a lot of water to develop their roots and leaves. They will only do well in moist soil. Water your plant preferably in the morning and afternoon with a watering can or by irrigation.

Figure 3-16: Watering plants in nursery

Staking

Some vegetables with long and weak stems, e.g. climbing beans, tomatoes, need stakes. A stake is a stick firmly put into the earth. It is best to use hard wood, which does not rot and can stay for some years.

Figure 3-17: Vegetables which have weak stems can be trained along stakes.

Pruning

Certain vegetables like tomatoes and eggplants need pruning. Nip off surplus buds. After pruning, there will be more fruits and they will be bigger.

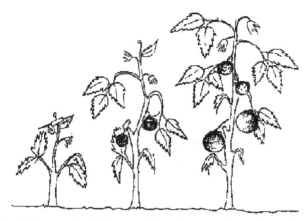

Figure 3-18: Pruned plants grow stronger and produce more fruit.

Garden care

The vegetables are frequently attacked by diseases and insects. There are chemical and natural methods to control insect and disease attacks. Chemical control is easier but expensive and risky. The poison of the chemical remains in the vegetable time between treatment and harvest is not long enough. You will then eat the chemical with the vegetable. Natural methods are more tedious and need a lot of observation and experience.

The easiest natural methods to control diseases are:

- Good seed/seedling selection disinfection of nursery bed (10 watering cans of boiling water for 10 m²) uprooting of infected plants and burning them
- Practicing mixed cropping; combine plants where the smell, etc. Of one plant affects or protects against diseases of the other plant, e.g. Tomato - cabbage, carrot – onion. In general, carrots, celery, onions, garlic, leeks are good partners to most of the other vegetables apart from pulses, e.g. Beans, peas, groundnuts, etc.
- Practicing crop rotation
- Putting sufficient manure to improve growth, because strong plants are more resistant to disease
- Choosing resistant or tolerant varieties

CHAPTER 4

HORTICULTURAL MACHINES & OPERATION

Content: Introduction to various horticultural machines, descriptions, utilization, and operations

4   Introduction

Horticultural machinery refers to any tool, implement and machine used in every stages of its operations. A wide range of horticultural machinery, tractors, stationary engine powered and tractor drawn/pulled equipment including cultivators, tractor mounted trimmers and mini-tractors etc have been employed among horticultural and gardening operations. Most popular innovation in the horticultural and gardening operations is the technological advancements in the design and manufacture of tractor powered and tractor drawn equipments used in horticultural operation. Few among such innovations are as discussed in the subsequent sections in this chapter.

4.2   Tractor and its features

The most popular types of tractors on farms and ranches today are the wheel tractors and crawler (chain) tractors.

Wheel tractors

Wheeled tractors generally have two large rear wheels with pneumatic tyres or ground-gripping metal lugs; they operate much like an automobile with a gearshift drive. Conventional wheeled tractor varies in sizes from tiny but effective models of 8-12.5 kW or less to large capacities of 260kW or more. In between these are various models and make of different layout and specifications.

Figure 4-1: Wheel tractor

Crawler (chain) tractors

Crawler tractors are used for heavy pulling or pushing or for adverse terrain conditions. These tractors move on heavy, metal tracks that form a loop around large geared wheels; the wheels drive the metal tracks, and the tracks distribute the weight over a wide area. Crawler tractors are well adapted to rough terrain, rice-land cultivation, and tillage operations in loose and sandy soil.

Figure 4-2: Crawler tractor

Lighter crawler tractors are frequently used for work on the sides of steep hills where they are less likely to overturn than wheeled tractors. The armored tank used in warfare is a military adaptation of the crawler tractor.

Advantages of crawler tractors

a. Good traction,
b. High power availability at draw bar,
c. Have lower operating cost.

Disadvantages of crawler tractors

a. High cost of procurement,
b. Poor maneuverability,

4.3   Tractor classification

Tractor classification refers to features that distinguish one tractor from the other. These features include the size (capacity) of tractor, locations of driving wheels and type of steering wheels. The various uses, adaptation and improvements of tractor brought about the evolution of several recognized classifications.

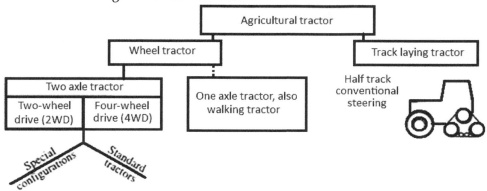

Figure 4-3: Tractor classification chart (CIGR, 1999)

Wheel tractors are generally classified either as one axle (power tiller or walking tractor) or two axle tractors.

4.3.1 One axle (power tiller) tractors

This is a two-wheeled tractor (better known as walking tractor or power/rotary tiller in Asia) guided by hand and is commonly designed for preparing garden beds. Small two wheel garden tractors, capable of cultivating and powering many useful attachments have been developed such as shown in Figure 4-4 below. When pushed along by hand, there are referred to as walk on and ride in when equipped with an attachment.

Figure 4-4: Power tiller

Power tillers are usually powered by 2.2-13 kW gasoline or diesel engines and are fitted with such features as rubber tyres or steel cage wheels with U shaped dual handle, automatic centrifugal clutch power drive, spiral cone-shaped gears etc. Other features include rear hitch system which made it to be used as ride on power tiller.

Figure 4-5: Power tillers used as ride-on

Uses of power tillers: They are used for soil working and seed-bed preparation by turning the soil over while breaking up large clods to ensure an even-textured planting bed. They are also used to loosen soils in new beds, to incorporate compost and other amendment into the soil, or to turn old crops into the soil at the end of the gardening season.

Mini tiller

Description: Multitudes of power tillers with powered attachments have been developed with minor improvements on the drive train. Such examples include the mini tillers. The working depth is adjustable up to 4 inches via moveable wheels and drag stake, tilling width is 6 to 10 inches.

Figure 4-6: Mini tiller (*Ardisam mc43*)

Uses: Mini tillers are designed for easy removal of weeds between plant rows and flower beds they are versatile in operation, easy to transport, featuring a carriage bar and foldable handles with accessories

Rotavator

Description: Rotavator is available in two versions: *push type* and *self propelled type* that picks up all kinds of car park or lawn debris. The self-propelled model uses a transmission system through an oil bath gearbox to hardened steel reduction gears at the wheels.

Figure 4-7: Rotavator

Uses: Many successful gardeners makes a choice of garden rotavator capable of braking the hard slog in the background and working up to a 60.5cm (24") digging width with a tough 5hp recoil start engine.

Power tiller operated auger digger

Description: Power tiller operated auger digger consists of a small frame with the provision to lower and raise the soil-working element. Drive is provided to the unit with the help of a set of bevel gears and belt pulleys. Lowering and raising the implement is accomplished by means of a rack and pinion arrangement which is operated by a hand wheel. It has two depth adjustment wheels, which support the weight of the implement, and provides stability.

Figure 4-8: Power tiller operated auger digger

In operation the auger is mounted on a power tiller and is lowered with the help of a steering. The auger is lifted when the desired depth of the hole is achieved.

Uses: Pits can be dug up to a depth of 45 to 60 cm and the diameter of the posthole is 30 cm. Suitable for digging circular pits for planting saplings. It is also suitable for use in orchards and forests due to its manoeuvrability

4.3.2 Two axle tractors

The two axle tractors are those tractors having four tyres; two tyres in front and two tyres at the rear axle. They are commonly classified based on two criteria as follows:

1. Type of drive wheel and
2. Functional classification

Each are further enumerated as follows

4.3.2.1   Classification of two axle tractors by drive wheels

Two types of tractor drive wheels are in common use today; two-wheel drives and four wheel drives. The two-wheel drive tractors have four wheels are arranged so that the two rear wheels are the power driving wheels while four-wheel drive tractors uses all the four wheels as power driving wheels.

a. Two-wheel drive tractors

Two-wheel drive tractors are two axle-tractors whose steering controls are powered by only the two front or rear wheels. Tractors in this class are generally divided into:

Standard tractors

Standard tractors are developed primarily for traction and are characterized by a drive through the two rear wheels, with center of gravity located at approximately one-third the wheel ahead of the rear axles.

Figure 4-9: Standard tractor with mounted row crop thinner

Standard tread tractor has fixed tread width and cannot be adjusted to meet different row widths. They have stability, rugged and simple design.

Row-crop tractors

Row crop tractors are essentially the conventional agricultural tractors suitable for traction works, adapted for the use on row crops, has quick attachment for various tillage tools etc. They provide greater under-tractor clearance along with provisions for adjusting the tractor tread width to match row crop spacing.

Figure 4-10: Row crop tractor with mounted row crop thinner

Low profile tractor

Low profile tractors are designed specifically for working in confined areas such as groves, orchards, within buildings etc. Examples of low profile tractors include

i. *Utility tractors*: Utility tractors have less clearance when compared with standard and row-crop tractors. They are often equipped with a front end loader and used for many jobs on the farm or ranch.

Figure 4-11: Utility tractor

ii. *Orchard tractor*: Orchard tractor is few centimeters lower in clearance than utility tractors. It is not equipped with roll-over-protective-structures (ROPS).

Figure 4-12: Orchard tractor

High clearance tractors

High clearance tractors has adjustable wide front axle with high clearance to cultivate tall crops such as sugar cane.

Figure 2-13: High clearance tractor

Advantages of 2- wheel drive

- Have smaller turning circle.
- Simplicity of design.
- Fewer mechanical parts.
- Lower purchase price

Disadvantages of 2- wheel drive

- Two wheel tractors have inability to work in wet and muddy conditions

b. *Four-wheel drive tractors*

Four-wheel tractors are classified into two basic types: Front wheel auxiliary drive and 'True' four-wheel drive.

i. *The front wheel auxiliary drive tractors* are basically the conventional gear-wheel tractors modified so that power may be sent to the front wheels when necessary.
ii. *'True' four-wheel drive tractors* have all the four wheels equal in size.

Advantages of 4-wheel drives

- Has ability to work in wet conditions
- Four-wheel drive tractors have excellent steering and traction characteristics in soft, wet fields.
- They are more efficient than the 2-wheel drive tractors

Disadvantages of 4-wheel drives

- Higher purchase and maintenance costs

4.3.2.2   Classification of two axle tractors by functions

Tractors suited for agricultural and horticultural operations are functionally classified as; agricultural tractors, compact tractors, lawn tractors and utility tractors.

1. *Agricultural tractors*

Description: An agricultural tractor is a self-powered work vehicle, designed for the purposes of pulling or pushing special machinery-moving or stationary (either off-road or on-road operation), or hauling of heavy loads over land. These are large, heavy-duty tractors suited for commercial farming.

Figure 4-14: Agricultural tractor

Uses: Agricultural tractors are widely used in agriculture, building construction, road construction, and for specialized services in industrial plants, railway freight stations, and docks.

2. *Compact tractors*

Description and uses: Compact tractors are smaller than agricultural tractors, less powerful or than utility tractors and suited for small, private farms. Compact tractors offer more functional capability than lawn-and-garden tractors and ATVs, and they can be equipped with necessary features, such as a PTO and three-point hitch, which most lawn-and-garden tractors lack.

Figure 4-15: Compact tractor (Kubota)

3. *Lawn tractors*

Description and uses: Conventional lawn tractors have a power output of less than 15kw and are primarily designed for the care of large lawns and not for agricultural production. A new range of multi-purpose garden tractors have been designed for horticultural purposes, residential and estate management requiring a power unit capable of operating a wide range of front and rear attachments.

Figure 4-16: MF 21-25 RD model lawn tractor

Rear discharge lawn tractor

Description and uses: These tractors are equipped additionally with rear discharge cutter decks with optional grass collection systems, heavy-duty welded tubular steel frames, pivoting front axles and pedal-engaged differential locks. They offer greater work capacity far greater than conventional lawn and garden tractors. Other specific features include selectable high and low speed ranges, power-assisted steering, electrically-engaged power take-off and dual hydraulic outlets at either the rear or both the front and rear of the machine. All these machines are powered by 25hp twin-cylinder petrol engines.

Figure 4-17: Rear discharge lawn tractor MF 21-25 RD model

An extensive list of options is available for these garden tractors, including turf or agricultural tyres, high-back seats and rear tipping grass collectors with electric or hydraulic opening. They are capable of cutting at a range of heights prior to mulching, collecting or discharging the clippings directly onto the ground. They offer comfort, power, manoeuvrability and speed work requires.

Side discharge lawn tractor

Description and uses: Tractors with side discharge are extraordinarily versatile. These machines with working widths of 96cm, 107cm or 127cm are characterised by optimal manoeuvrability on all models. Cutting the grass over larger areas is made quick and easy.

Figure 4-18: Side discharge lawn tractor

They are equipped with an easy to-operate cutting height adjustment and a suspended mowing deck for optimum cutting results even on difficult ground. Also, you can easily attach accessories, such as blades, lawn rollers or dump carts.

High grass cutting tractor

Description and uses: The high grass cutting deck tractor is especially suitable for use in wide expanse of land such as paddocks and meadows. They are equipped with traction agricultural tyres for even better grip on difficult mowing areas.

Figure 4-19: High grass cutting tractor (MF 36-22 HG)

Garden tractor

Description and uses: Garden tractors are designed with features like a 9-gauge welded-steel frame and a cast-iron front axle stand up to the toughest terrain. Plus, power steering makes it easy to operate the mower on all types of terrain.

Figure 4-20: Garden tractor

Ride-on mid mower

Description and uses: The new MF 50-24 IZ ride-on mid mower has independently-driven rear wheels and a unique steerable front axle operated by a conventional steering wheel. Drive to the two rear wheels is controlled by advanced synchro technology that synchronises front wheel steering movements with speed and direction of rotation of the rear wheels.

Figure 4-21: Zero turn ride-on tractor (MF 50-24 IZ)

The result is zero-turn radius agility from a conventionally steered mower, enabling 360 degree turns to be made within the length of the machine.

Figure 4-22: Zero turn ride-on tractor showing steering lock angle (MF 50-24 IZ)

Zero-turn front cut rotary rider

Description and uses: The front cut rotary riders such as MF 48-22 FMZ and MF 50-22 FMZ are using an advanced Synchro synchronised steering technology.

Figure 4-23: Zero turn front cut rotary rider (MF 48-22 FMZ)

These riders have front drive wheels whose speed and direction of rotation are controlled by movements of the rear steered axle, actuated through a conventional steering wheel.

Figure 4-24: Zero turn front-cut rotary rider (MF 50-22 FMZ)

The result is a high-output mower with a maximum working speed of 6 mph that is able to turn within its own length, delivering superb manoeuvrability, particularly useful for cutting in awkward or confined areas.

4. *Utility tractors*

Utility tractors are smaller, less powerful or both than agricultural tractors, but are heavy duty and usually sufficient for private farms and small commercial farming operations.

4.3.3 Utility vehicle and description

The general purpose utility vehicle is designed for work is equipped with several features for enhanced performance and job delivery. Among specialised features found in utility vehicles are; high ground clearance which allows the vehicle to negotiate rough terrains - including ridges and steps with ease, while the wet disc brakes provide smooth and consistent braking. They offer dynamic braking and automatic power boosts when climbing slopes. The fully hydrostatic power steering gives the operator the ease and manoeuvrability required.

Figure 4-25: Utility vehicle Kubota RTV900

4-wheel utility vehicles with fully independent double A-arm suspension and a wide stance offer increased stability on rough terrain while the 4x4 tight curb-to-curb turning circle and rear anti-roll bar provide superb cornering at faster speeds.

Figure 4-26: Carrying big loads with MF 20 MD 4x4 utility vehicle

More recently a number of all terrain utilities (ATUs) have emerged as having a role in some agricultural and horticultural production systems. The spreader shown in Figure below is a typical example of utility vehicle.

Figure4-27: All terrain utility (ATU) with spreader attachment

4.4   Ag bike and ATVs

The term 'Ag bike' also known as 'all terrain vehicles' or ATVs refers to all motorbikes with two, three or four wheels, used for garden and horticultural works. Small vehicles such as 2-wheeled motorcycles and 4-wheeled all terrain vehicles (ATVs) have become important to most agricultural production systems.

Figure 4-28: Ag bike/All terrain vehicles

Utilization of ATVs

ATVs are in widespread use on agricultural and horticultural farms. They are used for:

1. Personal travel around the farm
2. Mustering of livestock
3. Supervision of working field crews
4. Inspection of crops, pastures, fences, water and livestock
5. Towing and carrying of goods
6. Spraying of weeds
7. Shifting irrigation pipes
8. Markers for aerial operations
9. Recreation etc.

4.4.1   Ag bikes and descriptions

• *Cargo bicycle trailer*: This is a bicycle trailer designed for on road or off road transportation activities. The frame is powder coated steel to prevent rust, and is very heavy duty. The trailer tracks behind the bike perfectly and weighs about 22 lbs. It comes with removable and collapsible plastic bin.

Figure 4-29: Cargo bicycle trailer

4.5   Powered horticultural equipments

The most popular innovation in the horticultural and gardening operations is the technological advancements in the design and manufacture of powered equipments (either electrical or engine powered) used in horticultural operation. Few among such innovations are as discussed in the subsequent sections below.

4.5.1 Garden mowers

Grass mowing by machine varies from fine wicket or bowling-green to playing-fields and motorway embankments to crop field and jungle. Mowing is less recommended for handling cover crops, as the stubble of the cut cover crop could re-sprout. The first power tool to become popular with gardeners was the lawn mower which is manually or electrically powered.

Types of mowers

The different mowing machines can be grouped under headings:

a. *Rotating-disc mowers*: The rotating disc of the mower has a cutting mechanism of two or three replaceable high carbon steel blades travelling at high speed, cut through the grass on impact. The mechanism is either engine powered or driven by an electric motor. The height of cut can be adjusted by

   i.   Raising or lowering the land wheels,
   ii. Moving the rotating disc assembly up or down and
   iii. By the use of spacers or washers between the engine and the rotating disc.

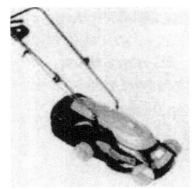

Figure 4-30: Rotating disc mower

b. *Cylinder mowers*: This group includes lawn mowers and gang mowers which are either hand propelled or tractor drawn. The cutting principle of cylinder mowers resembles that of a pair of scissors. The main components of cylinder mowers are:

i. *The cylinder*: The cylinder consisting of a number of spiral blades (3-12 blades) fastened to flanges mounted on a central shaft.

Figure 4-31: Cylinder mower

ii. *The bottom cutting blade*: The blade is a flat piece of steel varying in thickness from 3-6mm whose leading edge angle is less than 90°. The cutting blades are made of carbon steel and fastened to flanges mounted on a centre shaft. The spiral mounted cutting blades rotate, and cause progressive cutting action across the anvil blade.

iii. *Anvil stationary blade:* This is a stationary adjustable sharp edged flat blade made from high carbon steel positioned to trap grass in-between the high speed cutting blade and the stationary blade.. The grass is trapped between the rotating and anvil blades and cutting takes place due to shearing action.

iv. *Drive wheels*: The drive wheel provide required inertia to keep the blades working

v. *Rear and front-end roller assembly*: The rear roller provides the drive to the machine. In the hand driven type, the roller is roller is gear driven from the roller. The front roller is used to support the front end of the mower and allow for the height-of-cut adjustment.

c. *Flail mower:* This type is suitable for coarse grass or light scrub and is faster than reciprocating mower in action. Flail mowers are viewed as ideal mow-down equipment; they are equipped with optional caster wheels which can be raised when not required.

Figure 4-32: Flail mower

A horizontal rotor carry a number of swinging flails that turns at high speed up to 4000rpm. The flails have cutting edges that cut by impact. They swing out into their cutting position by centrifugal force. Flail mower knives rotate in a vertical plane. The removable discharge baffle allows the control of material output size while the roller offers height adjustment

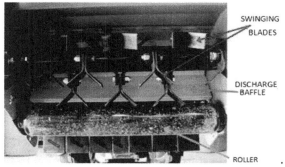

Figure 4-33: Underside of flail mower

d. *Hover mower:* This type of mower rides on a cushion of air and so does not need any wheels. A fan mounted on the crankshaft draws air through holes in the top of a hood and build up pressure which lifts the machine off the ground. This makes it very maneuverable and ideal for bank sides. The knife is a cutting bar with sharpened edges.

Figure 4-34: Hover mower

e. *Nylon-cord mowers* (commonly known as a "weed eater"): A piece of nylon cord is rotated at high speed and this pulverizes the grass and weeds on contact. The machine is electrically or engine powered. This mower is widely used for mowing in tight corners where it is difficult for other types of mowers.

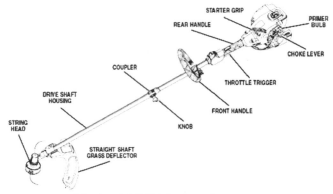

Figure 4-35: Nylon cord mower

f. *Reciprocating knife mower*: The knife reciprocates in the cutter bar and is driven by at the center by two lugs on the knife back. They might be driven by ground a wheel or they might use a small petrol engine. This type is less popular than the rotating-disc and the flail mower. They are normally equipped with cutter bars using reciprocating knives. However, animal draft mowers are very rarely used for cover crop management.

Manual/electrical operated lawn mowers

Manual and electric range lawn mowers are broadly used in various types of lawns cutting. Features of lawn mowers include cast iron frame, gear and pinion transmission system, two to six cutting cylinder blades running on ball bearings in dust proof housing, specially blade strengthened lipped cutting edge for height durability, variable handle, tubular steel, self adjustable to height of the operator and variable cutting height adjustment from 3/4 to 2 inches.

Figure 4-36: Lawn mowers: electrical and manual

Lawn mowers that are ideal for maintaining small lawns, are made of aluminum die casted wheels which delivers outstanding power coupled with high performance gear system, economy in working, a corrosion - resistant that will never rust, ball bearing wheels for smooth maneuvering and a catcher with metal lining for added durability

Self propelled lawn mowers

Self propelled lawn mowers is a display of modern technology and the best workmanship see to it that powerful engine, the easy to- empty grass bag, the ergonomically formed handle and the easy-to-handle cutting height adjustment guarantee excellent mowing results.

Figure 4-37: Self propelled mower (MF 21 SHWB)

There are different ways to dispose the clippings: either through mulching, bagging or discharge. When using for mulching, the grass clippings are cut several times to fine particles and can directly be used as a natural green fertilizer.

Scythe mowers

Power scythes are the perfect machines for clearing work and are capable of performance whatever the conditions. The system is ideal for cutting and opening up areas up to about three to four acres. Cutter bar mowers cut down material at the base like a big scissors, and leave the material whole. It comes fitted with an engine, and a unique design of cutting bar which totally eliminates clogging. Some scythes models cuts vegetation up to 1" diameter, with the engine just above tick over which means they will run all day on just one full tank of fuel.

Figure 4-38: Scythe mower (BCS 615SL)

These mowers had evolved from the single-action lower blade design which cuts right through a hay-bale without clogging to the latest innovation of "double-action" units which has the upper and lower blade assemblies that both reciprocate opposite each other to cancel out at least 95% of the vibrations, which are the most objectionable part of using a walk-behind cutter bar mower. The double-action bars also come with spring-loaded blade tensioners.

Lawn aerator

Good aeration is the key to any high quality lawn, reducing soil compaction, and increasing water sorption, which will give you the healthy looking lawn you are after. Powered by a top IC engine for maximum performance and reliability, the offset crank operating system allows the power of the engine to punch the tines into the ground resulting in perfect aeration.

Figure 4-39: Lawn aerator (LA20Professional Petrol Aerator)

4.5.2 Garden sweepers

Hand propelled floor sweeper

Hand propelled floor sweeper, uses a multi-clean sweeping system to sweep up all kinds of debris. The intelligent sweeping concept prevents even large bits of debris from getting stuck under the tool. It has a central height adjustment, ideal for use on different floor surfaces. There is a durable nylon bristles, ideal for sweeping around the outside of the lawn.

Figure 4-40: Floor sweeper with 25 litre collector *(Stihl kg550)*

Push leaf sweeper

Description: With a clearing width of 25" (over 65cms), this height-adjustable, lightweight, leaf and debris sweeper with large easy-running 10" (25.5cm) diameter wheels is simply suitable for collecting masses of fallen leaves from lawns or paths and will save untold hours of sweeping, raking and back-breaking stooping. It is powered by simply walking and gently pushing along without any electric cable to worry about plugging in.

Figure 4-41: Push leaf sweeper (Eckman)

The sweeper's heavy duty, nylon coated rotating brushes are powered by a gearing system taken from rotation of the wheel axle. The brushes have different height settings making the sweeper suitable for different surfaces. Leaf or grass cutting debris are all swiftly collected in the rot-resistant collection bag for fewer visits to the green recycling or compost bin.

Figure 4-42: Push leaf sweeper (Eckman)

Uses: Collect a huge amount of leaves from lawns or paths by simply pushing the sweeper along

Tow-behind lawn sweeper

Description: Tow-behind lawn sweeper collects leaves and grass clippings with a built in powerful brushes for a clean sweep the first time through. It has wide sweeping brush that ensures a one pass performance with extra large hamper provided. It has compact storage either hanging or standing upright with an exclusive self storing feature.

Figure 4-43: Leaf sweeper

John Deere 42-inch, 24 cubic feet hanger capacity tow-behind lawn sweeper has a 50 in. W x 53 in. D x 28 in. H assembled dimension and high tip brush velocity. The brushes develop enough force required to move object off the ground and into the hamper storage. It has six 11 inch-diameter brushes compared to 4 brush designs

Figure 4-44: John Deere tow-behind lawn sweeper

The Agri-Fab 38-inch tow-behind lawn sweeper used with a garden tractor or an ATV has 4 to 10 inch diameter brushes that are replaceable. Additionally the 10 x 1 3/4 inch tires are semi-pneumatic. This Agri-Fab boasts "infinite" height adjustments making it easy to find just the right height for most lawns and grass lengths. One great aspect of this lawn sweeper is that it is easy to assemble

Figure 4-45: Agri-Fab 38-inch is a tow-behind lawn sweeper

Uses: Users have noted that sweeper is better used for dry leaves, larger pine needles, small pine cones and dry grass. Although picking up anything wet seems to be hard work for this sweeper.

Leaf vacuum, blower and shredder

Description: This is a powerful, lightweight, easy-to-maneuver 3-in-1 vacuum leaf cleaning equipment equipped with an extra wide suction head and front blower and shredder from Eckman that clears garden of fallen leaves in a fraction of the time and effort it takes if were required to rake and sweep the leaves. The equipment also has features to also shred those collected leaves by up to 90% of their original size, producing extra fast-rotting compost material for digging back into flower beds, vegetable plots or for spreading on as mulch.

Figure 4-46: Push leaf sweeper (Eckman)

This equipment has other features such as extra wide 18½" (47cm) main suction head, front blower to clear leaves off gravel pathways, quick switch from vacuum to blower mode, 25-litre collection bag and adjustable height for variable terrain e.g. grass to concrete path

Uses: If you have a lot of debris you need picked up fast and easily, you definitely want to check out a leaf vacuum. Leaf vacuums are amazing in that, some models will pick up everything from rocks, bottles, trash, and not to mention leaves!

Self propelled litter vacuums

Description: Self propelled litter vacuums features a large 5-blade impeller with serrated edges, variable height adjustment integral dust skirt, optional hose kit zipperless bag and self-propelled by a 190 cc Briggs (KV600, KV600SP) or 187 cc Honda (KV650H, KV650SPH, TKV650SPH) engine. The bag volume capacity is 40 gal.

Figure 4-47: Push leaf sweeper (Eckman)

4.5.3 Garden shredders and scarifier

Power slider disc shredder

Description: The electric powered slider disc garden shredders has such features as the plastic housing to keep the noise levels low, suitable for work in built up areas. Improved design of hopper allows for easy feeding with a large opening. The opening provides kickback-free feeding with a guiding plate that directs material straight into the cutting blades minimising risk of clogging.

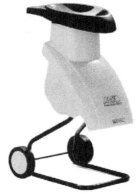

Figure 4-48: Electric power slider disc shredder (Alko power slider 2500)

Usage: The electric powered slider disc garden shredders are designed for small to medium sized gardens and use modern materials resistant to corrosion for a long working life.

Tractor mounted brush cutters

The operating width of brush cutter varies with design and manufacturer, for instance, the D-514A brush cutter with two horizontal blades manufactured in the USSR is 3.6 m wide, and its productivity is up to 0.6 hectares per hr. It is used for cutting brush and small trees with diameters between 50 and 300 mm. The brush cutter operates with a T-100MGP tractor in second gear.

Uses: A brush cutter is one of the most versatile tools for clearing brush and small trees from areas when preparing land for agricultural crops, clearing routes for the construction of roads and canals, and setting up forest cuttings.

Debris loaders

Description: Comparing with other truck loaders, debris loaders are designed to shreds and moves debris on the lawn. Debris loaders have been designed for ease of use with a higher reduction and competition rate.

Figure 4-49: Heavy duty debris loader (Subaru, e/start.)

The DL such features as electric start petrol engine which is coupled to an 18", 6-bladed, armoured plated impeller with 18 cutting points, for up to a 12:1 reduction ratio. This unit also features a convenient replaceable poly liner for the housing.

A large clear poly helical hose is ideal for taking huge bites out of any debris pile. A hand crank adjusts the exhaust through 360 degrees of rotation without using tools. There is an optional trailer available which has a small footprint for easy towing and storage.

Scarifier

Description: The scarifier is a compact machine for weed control. It has compact size and is lightweight making it easy to manoeuvre, the handles fold right down allowing for easy storage. The machine has a working width of 30cm and features a powerful 1100watt induction motor, cutting system, blades, and heights of cut adjuster which is controlled by a single lever.

Figure 4-50: Electric scarifier (wolf cp1000v)

Weed control by scarifying with electric scarifier is easy and are amongst the best technologies available.

Usage: When in use, it will free your lawn of thatch and moss and promote healthier looking lawns.

Trenchers

Description: The special feature of this implement is to form deep channels by removing the sub-soil from the land surface. Trenches are usually dug manually by employing labour which results to enormous amount during compost and other inorganic fertilizer application to tree crops can be eliminated by fixing this implement to a tractor. This implement is suitable to be attached to 30, 35, 40, 45 and 50 HP tractors.

Figure 4-51: Mini trencher

Uses: The self-propelled mini trencher is used for landscape trenching applications such as trenching of soil for sprinkler systems. This implement is also useful for digging pits and canals to lay pipelines for drip irrigation system. It is possible to dig long trenches and canals for applying fertilizers with less cost. During the rainy season, by providing channels for the disposal of waste water with this implement, it is possible to save the crop from the excess rain water.

Posthole digger

Description: Posthole digger is an attachment to the three-point linkage of tractor. It consists of an auger, which is driven through bevel gears. The auger gets drive from the tractor PTO through a propeller shaft and bevel gear box. The perpendicularity of digging auger is maintained with four-bar linkage formed by hitching system the tie rod provided at the top, The tip of the auger is either; diamond shaped or pointed with wings to suit to different soil conditions. The diameter and depth of hole can be changed by changing the auger assembly.

Figure 4-52: Posthole digger

Uses: To dig holes for planting tree saplings

4.5.4 Garden rollers

Tractor drawn garden rollers

Description: Garden roller is agricultural as well as gardening equipment with rollers powered by an engine for multi-applications. *Lawn rollers* for heavy duty applications are tractor drawn with a draw bar attachment point, 36" wide and 18" diameter roller.

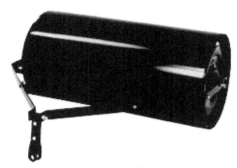

Figure 4-53: Push/pull roller (tractor drawn)

Uses: Garden roller is used to flatten land or breaking up large lumps of soil after ploughing is done. Garden rollers are used in applications where there is a requirement of having flat land or surface for undertaking any kind of activity. Garden rollers are also used in sowing seeds and press seeds into the soil for better germination process. Another application of garden rollers is in sports stadiums and pitches. Garden rollers are widely used for producing lawn stripes in cricket, tennis or other playgrounds.

4.6   Soil cultivation equipment

Tractors, and to a lesser extent power tillers, are used with a wide range of implements, of which some are designated for secondary tillage, (i.e. spike harrows, disc harrows and multi-purpose toolbars) and some designated for primary tillage (i.e. disc ploughs, mouldboard ploughs, rotary cultivators and weeders).

4.6.1 Primary tillage implements

The implement most often used for primary tillage with tractors include

1.   Mouldboard plough,
2.   The disc plough; less common are
3.   Rotary cultivators and
4.   Power tillers mounted with a rotary cultivator or a ploughing body.
5.   Other tools in use include chisel plough, sub-soiler and rotary tillers.

Mouldboard plough

The design of the mouldboard, like the size and form, determines the quantity of crop residues that is left on the surface and the part that is mixed into the soil. The bigger and more curved the mouldboard the higher the amount of the residues that is inverted in the soil and thus fewer residues that are left on the surface.

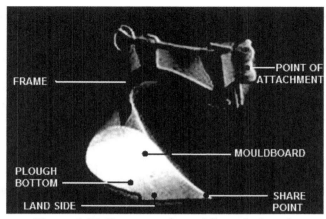

Figure 4-54: Features of mouldboard plough

Component part of mouldboard plough

1. *Carrier frame*: The frame carries the mouldboard bottom and it is attached to the tractor through the 3-point –hitch.

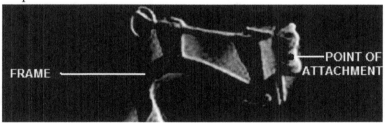

Figure 4-55: Frame carrier

2. *Plough bottom*: consists of mould board, share, land side and standard or frog.

   a. *Mouldboard* lifts and turns (inverts) the cut furrow slice. In sticky soils, strip moldboards can help to reduce draft forces since they have a smaller surface subject to adhesion.

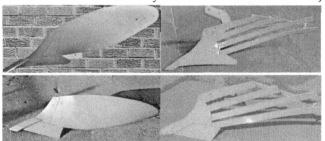

Figure 4-56: Mouldboards

   b. The *share*: The horizontal cut of the furrow slice is made by the share which is rectangular in shape and acts like a wedge, forcing its way through the soil lifting as well as cutting. The share is designed to penetrate the soil by what is known as *share pitch* and to pull into the unploughed land by *lead-to-land*. Share point cuts the furrow slice open.

Figure 4-57: Mouldboard share

c. The *landside*: Usually made of steel, presses against the furrow walls and absorb the side thrust of the plough. The rear landside is usually larger than the others and has a wearing part at its end called the *heel*.

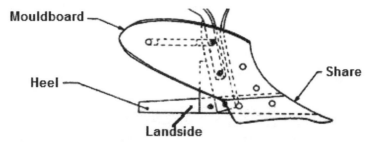

Figure 4-58: Landside

d. *The frog* is steel or cast iron attached to the bottom of the leg and is used as a mounting for all the soil working parts that make the body. It stabilizes the plough and absorbs shock. Pulverization is promoted if the mould curvature is such as to produce simultaneous movement of all primary shear planes as the implement move forward.

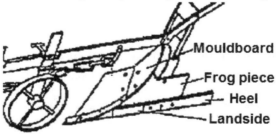

Figure 4-59: The frog

3. *Axles* and wheels depending on type of plough
4. The *coulter* makes a vertical cut through the unploughed land in the forward direction. This is either a knife or a disc which is free to rotate. Scrapes away soils attached to the mould bottom in a non-scouring soil.

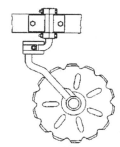

Figure 4-60: Disc coulter

5. *The skin coulter* scrapes away soils attached to the mould bottom in a non-scouring soil. Scouring is the movement of soil across a tool surface without sticking and fast enough to avoid soil build up.
6. *The skimmer*: Skimmers are fitted to the disc coulters so that surface trash can be buried completely. The skimmer is usually set to pare off a corner of the furrow slice and direct it unto the bottom of the furrow, while the mouldboard turns the furrow slice on top.

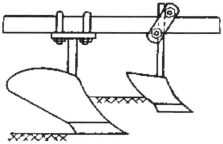

Figure 4-61: The skimmer

Disc plough

This is used in hard soil where the mouldboard plough could not penetrate; especially in wet, sticky soil condition, in stony and stumpy fields and in soil containing a lot of buried roots, hence particularly preferred in Nigeria, especially in Southern Nigeria.

Disc plough depends on their weights for penetration hence heavier than mouldboard plough. Weight per disc blade is between 1.75-3.35KN, and spherical radius of curvature is 45-60 cm. Depth of cut depends on; blade diameter, disc angle and width of cut. Disc plow can be one way or reversible in arrangement.

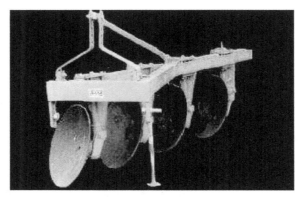

Figure 4-62: 4 wheel disc plough

Types of disc plough

There are different types of disc plough used in specific field conditions and include;

1. One-way disc plough
2. Offset disc plough and
3. Tined plough implements.

Others include universal disc, hare disc and the rotary type disc plough.

1. *One-way disc plough:* The one way disc plough is used in 2-wheel and 4-wheel tractor powered systems. The number and size of disc shares vary according to the power source. 2-wheel tractors will use 2 or 3 disc ploughs, while a 4-wheel tractor will pull 3, 4 or 7 disc versions. Disc plough depends on their weights for penetration hence heavier than mouldboard plough.

Figure 4-63: *Disc plough used in with 2-wheel tractor*

The disc plough causes total inversion of the soil sod and relies on the ploughs in built weight for penetration. Weight per disc blade is between 1.75-3.35KN, and spherical radius of curvature is 45-60 cm.

2. *Offset disc plough:* As the name implies, this is a plough that is capable of operating offset from the tractor. The plough is made up of between four and twenty-four discs mounted in two gangs. Each gang has a common center bolt and throws the soil in different direction. These ploughs are only used on 4-wheel tractors and are very versatile. An offset plough can be operated in any ploughing pattern. The offset plough can be either 3-point linkage mounted or a trailing version.

Figure 4-64: Offset disc for 4-wheel tractor

Mouldboard/disc plough comparison

Mouldboard differs from a disc plough in the following ways

S/N	Factors	Mould board	Disc plough
1.	*Cutting edge*	Presence of share point	Disc cutting edge
2.	*Disc shape*	Mould board oval in shape	Disc concave in curvature
3.	*Stability*	Land side present	Disc coulter present
4.	*Mode of operation*	Slides through soil	Cut through soil
5.	*Resistance*	Cut through obstacle	Rolls over hard pan

Rotary cultivator

The best known and most universal driven tillage machine is the rotary cultivator (Figure 4-51), whose use ranges from primary and secondary tillage in conventional systems to minimum (conservation) tillage and use in paddy field rice cropping.

Figure 4-65: Rotary cultivator

The cultivator consists of a horizontal rotor which is equipped with various kinds of tines, spikes or knives (Figure 4-65). The action of the tool is to beat or cut along the whole tine length, and thus is more aimed at crumbling clods, while the rotary cultivator cuts typical bites out of the soil. The mixing abilities are still rather good. Using tines or spikes causes a considerable reduction in the power requirement compared to a rotary tiller.

Rotary plough

The principle of combination of plough with rotating implements was realized in the powered disk plow. It is actually a disk harrow using comparatively large disks which are rotated by the tractor PTO in order to ease cutting of the soil and reduce draft forces.

The disks are indented or can be equipped with additional tines, which perform further crumbling of the turning soil. By driving the disks, the formation of a hardpan can be avoided. As the machine needs both PTO and drawbar power without creating a seedbed, this is a machine only for especially difficult and wet soil conditions.

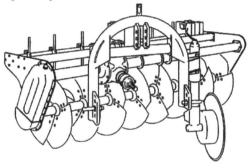

Figure 4-66: PTO driven disk plough

Spading machine

Another driven tillage machine is the spading machine (Figure 4-52). It imitates the manual work of digging with a spade. The advantage is that this machine forms almost no hardpan as the path of the tools in the soil is almost never parallel to the soil surface. But the machine is rather complicated and comparatively energy consuming.

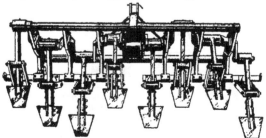

Figure 4-67: Spading machine

Tine/chisel plough

Chisels plough are sharply pointed, metal tines that can be attached to ordinary plough beam. Usually, farmers who want to avoid ploughing in minimum or reduced land preparation activities use chisels.

Figure 4-68: Animal drawn chisel plough (T. Friedrich)

Chisel plough can also be used to break up plough pans or other impermeable soil layers, like crusts. A typical example of animal drawn chisel plough is shown in Figure 4-54. As a first step to convert from conventional plough based farming towards conservation agriculture, farmers might opt for tined implements such as chisel plough or cultivator.

Disadvantages of chisel plough include:

1. Poor weed control
2. Requires adequate soil condition (at crumbling point or dryer) to work properly
3. Residues and vegetation on the surface clogs up the implement
4. Lifting stones and clods

Subsoiler

Subsoilers are primary tillage heavy-duty implement used in breaking up hard or compacted soil layers, with the aim of improving water infiltration and root penetration. It can be attached to the ordinary plough beam. It can also be used to break up dry soil. The point is brought right under the compacted layer and can be used up to soil depths of 25-60cm.

Figure 4-69: Narrow and pointed chisel subsoilers

With animal traction the maximum working depth of a chisel is around 30 cm. For this reason real subsoiling is not possible with animals, but shallow compactions can be broken using adequately shaped chisels.

4.6.2 Secondary tillage implement

Secondary tillage implies the preparation of a seedbed after the first coarse primary tillage. Normally an implement that is used for primary tillage will not be used again for secondary tillage. Again, tractors, and to a lesser extent power tillers, are used with a wide range of implements, of which some are designated for secondary tillage, (i.e. spike harrows, disc harrows and multi-purpose toolbars) and some are not (i.e. disc ploughs, mouldboard ploughs, rotary cultivators and weeders).

Functions of secondary tillage

Further tillage operation is carried out following primary tillage for any of the following reasons;

1. To further develop a seedbed by pulverizing soil clod
2. To form top soil for better moisture movement
3. To cut up crop residue and mix vegetative matter or other materials into the top soil
4. To destroy or control weeds.

Secondary tillage tool

In conventional tillage systems, the seedbed is typically prepared in a second step. This creates a fine seedbed on the loosened soil left by primary tillage.

Drawn secondary tillage tools

Drawn secondary tillage tools can be used easily for great working widths at high working speeds. They create a stratified seedbed and are comparatively simple and cheap. Their great advantage is that the intensity of work usually increases with working speed. On more difficult soils, together with mulch or under wet conditions, the use of drawn secondary tillage tools is limited.

Floats

Floats (Figure 4-70) are amongst the most simple secondary tillage tools. They are pulled over the soil surface without engaging implements in the soil. Their effect is mainly leveling, and they are used to grade ridges or ruts from previous crops. At the same time, they have a certain crumbling and mixing effect.

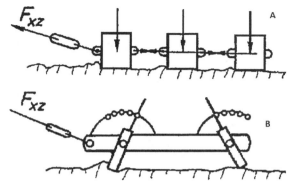

Figure 4-70: Floats; fixed version (A) and adjustable version right (B)

Disc harrow

Disc harrow can either be plain with regular contour or notched (scallop) for pasture removal *and* cutting of heavy trash. Tractor mounted disc harrows were developed after the advent of tractor mounted tools and it is popular for certain applications. Their weights are limited because they have to be lifted by tractor. Advantage includes easy maneuverability and ease of transportation. A disc of a harrow implement has less concavity than the disc of a plough implement. Increasing the concavity of the disc will enable better turning of the soil but at the expense of depth penetration.

Figure 4-71: A fully mounted disc harrow

Classification of disc harrow

Classification of disc harrow is based on the arrangement of gangs as follow:

Single action disc harrow: This has two opposed gang of disc blade both throwing dirt out from the center of tilt. Width of gang is 3.048m.

Figure 4-72: Single action disc harrow

Double action (tandem): Two single action disc harrows are arranged in opposing direction to achieve better and even breaking of the soil. Soil is turned twice leaving the soil well pulverized. Figure 4-73 shows double action disk harrow in half transport position and half working position.

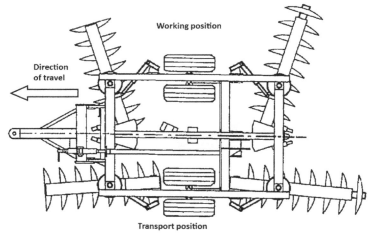

Figure 4-73: Double action disc harrow

Offset disc harrow: This has one right gang which moves the soil to the right and one left gang operating in tandem with it. The forces acting upon an offset disc harrow are such that when it is operating with low side graft, the center of the tilt strip is considerably to one side of pull and usually that width of such cut is between 4.5-12ft. This arrangement overcomes the problem of tilt strip of the front gang and it also leaves the soil or field in relatively even condition if properly adjusted.

Spike tooth harrow

This is lying flat on the field with spikes (teeth) underneath working to a depth of 5cm. It thoroughly smoothes and compacts the top soil, fill up large air spaces left from ploughing and breaks up lumps and clods, used for pre–emergence cultivation to break the rain- formed crust and destroy small weeds

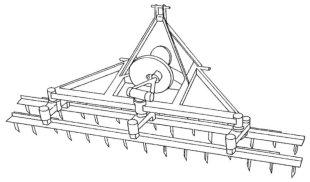

Figure 4-74: A reciprocating spike tooth harrow

Coiled (spring) tine harrow

This is spike tooth harrow with coiled tines. It breaks the soil crust and penetrates as deep as 18cm.

Figure 4-75: Coiled (spring) tine Harrow

It mixes trash and stubble used for pasture, Orchard and vineyard cultivation. Harrow teeth are usually 44cm wide 7.8-15.9mm thick.

Mulcher

This is a combination of spring cultivator teeth to dig up clods and pulveriser (with rough surface to break the clods). They are equipped with land rollers to support the frame in operation.

Rotary tillage tools

Another variety of drawn secondary tillage machines includes those with rotating implements. These implements equipped with cutter bars, spikes, or teeth are attached to a wheel or roller, and are thus penetrated into the soil. Bars usually cut the soil while the tines or spikes have an effect on the penetrated soil and tend to break it into crumbles. Beside this, the spikes do mix soil and residues. This is especially true if the tines are combined with a disk (e.g., the rotary spade harrow shown in Figure 4-76).

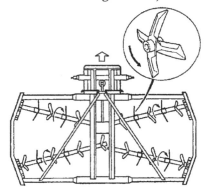

Figure 4-76: Rotary spade harrow

Simpler machines are varieties of spiked rotors (Figure 4-77), which just roll over the soil surface.

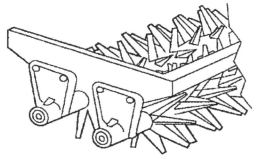

Figure 4-77: Spiked rotor

To increase the levering and crumbling effect of such rotors, a machine with two rotors was designed, the Dyna-drive (Figure 4-78). It consists of two rotors, which are joined by a chain drive.

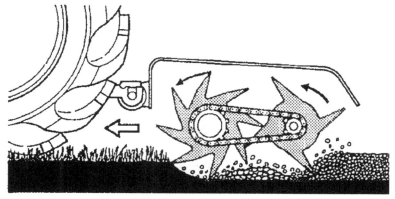

Figure 4-78: Dyna-drive spiked rotor

The gear ratio from the first to the second rotor is 1: 2 up to 1: 3. Thus, the first rotor drives the second rotor. The effect of the first rotor mainly is to break and loosen the soil, and it works best if it finds some resistance breaking up settled soil, while the second rotor performs crumbling and mixing.

Rotovators

Rotovators consist of a horizontal rotor which is equipped with various kinds of tines, spikes or knives (Figure 4-79). The action of the tools is to beat or cut along the whole tine length, and thus is more aimed at crumbling clods, while the rotary cultivator cuts typical bites out of the soil.

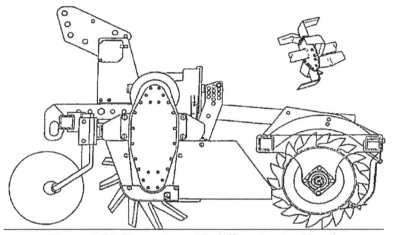

Figure 4-79: Rotovator with different rotor (inset)

The mixing abilities are still rather good. Using tines or spikes causes a considerable reduction in the power requirement compared to a rotary tiller. This means it can be used with some success in settled soils for stubble cleaning or mulching, and it is very important machinery for reduced tillage.

Power harrows

A rather important PTO-driven machine for secondary tillage especially for heavy soils is the rotary harrow (Figure 4-80). It consists of a number of rotating disks, which are usually equipped with two or three tines that are angled towards the soil. Thus, they mainly beat and crush clods on the soil surface and press them into the soil. During the operation of the rotary harrow, a wall of earth builds up before the machine but due to the horizontal movement of the tools, almost no mixing occurs. This earth wall creates a level plane surface after the passage of the machine. Compared to the rotovator, the energy consumption is higher.

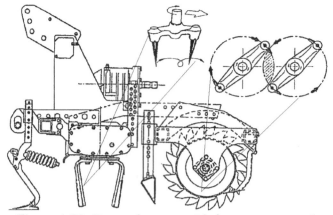

Figure 4-80: Rotary harrow with furrow press tool

Disk ridger

This tool is designed for making irrigation ridges, terraces and beds. It consists of a two 3-blade rotary disk gangs rotating on pressure-lubricated, anti-friction bearings. Each gang has full range of adjustment, both for soil throw and for angle of cut. They work well in heavy clay as well as loose, well-prepared soils.

Figure 4-81: A 2- blade disk ridger

Border disk plough

Light draft border disk plough builds high, well-shaped irrigation checks and borders. Disks (28-inch diameter) turn easily on double tapered roller bearings that are pressure-lubricated.

Figure 4-82: Border disk plough

Irrigation furrower

Irrigation furrower is designed to make deeper irrigation furrows, and to work in harder soils.

Tillers

This equipment is used for field cultivation, stubble mulching, digging and breaking up of hard-packed soil faster than Sub-soiler, but works at shallow depths. The double coiled shanks with reversible point shovels penetrate the soil with a vibrating action.

Figure 4-83: Double rigid shank tiller

4.7   Spraying system, equipment and calibration

The sprayer is one of the most common machines used to apply liquid chemicals for weed and insect control. They are important equipment for pesticide applications. Examples are knapsack sprayers (hand operated), boom sprayer (tractor mounted). However, some sprayers operated in the air through helicopter or airplane for large hectares of land.

Sprayer components

A basic field spraying system typically consists of the following components:

1. *A tank* to hold a mixture of active chemical ingredient(s) and water;
2. *A centrifugal pump:* This accelerate the rate of flow of chemicals through the hose
3. *Throttling/shut-off valves;* These devices controls the rate of fluid flow into the nozzle
4. *A boom:* This is a large capacity reservoir mounted on tractor for chemical mixture
5. *Nozzle:* The nozzle is used for controlling application rate, uniformity and surface area of application. The nozzle performs three main functions on the sprayer:

a. Regulates flow;
b. Atomizes the mixture into droplets; and
c. Disperses the spray in a specific pattern.

Nozzle spray pattern: The shape of the spray pattern is the third function that nozzles perform. Each pattern has two characteristics, the spray angle and the shape of the pattern. The typical spray angle is 65°, 80°, 110° or 120° to 130°. The shape of the pattern can be reduced to a basic three: the flat fan, the hollow cone and the solid cone (Figure 4-70).

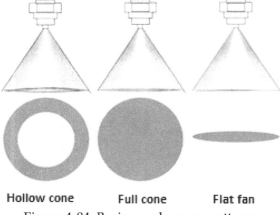

Hollow cone   Full cone   Flat fan

Figure 4-84: Basic nozzle spray patterns.

6. *Strainers:* Used for preventing large particles from clogging in the small orifice of thee tip and
7. *Control system* which includes pressure gauge and control values. *The pressure gauge* is a graduated dial scale used to measure the force exerted per unit area of tank
8. *The plumbing pipes* and hoses necessary to connect the components for liquid transfer from tank to nozzles. This also includes hydraulic agitators and control valves;

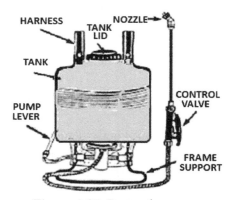

Figure 4-85: Parts of sprayer

Control valves: Valves are vital to proper functioning of sprayers. Some typical valves in sprayers include;

a. *Relief valves:* These limit the maximum pressure of the sprayer and prevent damage. In addition to limiting pressure,

b. *The unloader valve* unloads the pump (full flow at low pressure) to save energy and wear when the sprayer is idling and not calling for sprayer discharge.

c. *Throttling valves* are used to control the amount of flow volume and boom selector valves control the active section of the sprayer boom.

d. *Flow control valves* are available as manual or as electric valves.

Sprayer classification

Sprayers fall into four major categories as described in section 2.2.3 under plant protection tools and description (pages 26-39).

4.7.1 Sprayer calibration

Many methods are available for calibrating sprayers, but some are easier to use than others. Two methods that work well are given here. All calibration techniques rely on three variables that affect the amount of spray applied per hectare: the nozzle flow rate, the ground speed, and the effective width of each nozzle. Any change in one of these variables will have a direct effect upon the others.

Sprayers can be calibrated in three ways

1. Field calibration and
2. Experimental calibration
3. Timed-flow method

The following methods can be used in calibration depending on field or experimental processes.

1.   Sprayer calibration using field method

To calibrate a sprayer, make a trial run on a field or turf area and measure the variables with your chosen equipment. This process gets the right quantity of chemical to be applied on the right size of field.

Note: always use pure water to calibrate your equipments.

A standard boom requires between 220-225 ltr/hectares of chemical.

Calibration procedure

Step 1: Fill the tank with water, mount on tractor and select the right gear speed e.g. gear 2 at 540 rpm and a speed 8 km/hr will spray between 220-225 ltr/ hectare.

Step 2: Map out a portion of your field say (100 x 10) m² (1/10) ha. The width of your boom determines this. Assume the width of about 10m.

Step 3: Fill the tank to capacity either graduated or not graduated.

Step 4: Spray across the entire area and measure the quantity remaining in the tank.

Step 5: The quantity measured multiplied by 10 will give the quantity sprayed per hectare.

2. *Sprayer calibration using experimental method*

Experimental calibration is required to obtain the correct distribution of chemical by evaluating the speed of travel and the pressure setting that will be used by the operation in the field. Experimental calibration can be done in two ways as follows:

Method 1: volume-distance method

Calibration procedure

Step 1: Measure a distance of 201m on the level surface and state

Step 2: Drive spray rig over the 201m courses at the same speed that will be used on the field. Measure and record time accurately.

Step 3: Move the rig to a level spot and set the brakes.

Step 4: Operate the sprayer at the pressure that will be used on the field.

Step 5: Catch the discharges from 3 or 4 nozzles (one nozzle from each boom of a 3-boom rig) for the exact length of time that it took to travel the 201m in *step* 2 above.

Step 6: Record the liquid volumes obtained from the test nozzle and calculate the volume that would have been delivered by all nozzles as follows:

Volume applied over 201m in (gal)

$$V = \frac{V_c \; x \; N}{n} \; (ltr) \; .... 4.1$$

Where
 V = Volume applied
 Vc =Volume Caught (ltr)
 N= No. of nozzles or sprayers

n = Number of nozzle used in test.

(Conversion factor 1 gallon = 4.55ltr)

Method 2: Area load-volume method

In another method of calibration, the area load-volume method, the principle is to apply a known volume of chemical over a known area. The application rate is then calculated as the volume divided by the area. This application rate is then multiplied by the nutrient concentrations of the manure to determine the amount of nutrients applied to the area. This information can then be used to adjust the manure application rate to meet the crop's requirements.

Calibration procedure

Step 1: Determine the sprayer tank capacity in gallons. If the tank's capacity is in cubic feet use the conversion rate of 7.5 gal per cuft = 1gal.

Example: 400 cuft x 7.5 gal/cuft = 3000 gal (13,638.27ltr)

Step 2: Spread one or more loads of manure to the field. The manure should be applied using the same equipment settings, ground speed, swath width and pattern overlap that will be used in normal application practices.

Example: 1 load applied at 1.5 mph (2.4km/h)

Step 3: Measure and calculate the land area to which the manure was applied. The application area should be square or rectangular so you can multiply the length and width to calculate the land area. The distances can be determined by measuring or pacing.

Example: 100 ft (30.48m) wide x 200 ft (60.96m) long = 20,000 sqft (1858.06 m²)

Step 4: Convert the area from step 3 to acres using the conversion rate of 43,560 sqft per acre.

Example: 20,000 sqft ÷ 43,560 sqft/ac = 0.46 ac

Step 5: The application rate is calculated as the tank capacity from step 1 times the number of loads from step 2 divided by the application area in acres from *step* 4.

Example: 3, 000 gal x 1 load ÷ 0.46 ac = 6,522 gal/ac

Step 6: The pounds (kg weight) of nutrients applied per acre (hectare) is calculated by multiplying the gallons per acre (ltr/ha) applied from step 5 by the pounds of nutrient per 1,000 gallons of wastewater and then dividing by 1,000.

Example: 6, 522 gal/ac x 20 lb N/1000 gal ÷ 1000 = 130 lb N/ac

3. *Timed-flow method for calibrating boom sprayers*

This is an excellent method that gets you close to the needed nozzle size and flow rate quickly and easily. This calibration procedure allows you, the grower, to make the management decisions of: 1) the type of nozzle to use (based upon experience and preference); 2) the rate per hectare to apply; 3) the travel speed of the sprayer; and 4) the nozzle spacing on the boom. Using these variables in the equation below, the size of the nozzle is calculated and then identified in the appropriate nozzle catalog.

$$N \ (l/min) = \frac{A \left(\frac{l}{ha}\right) \ x \ S \left(\frac{km}{hr}\right) \ x \ W \ (cm)}{60,000} \quad \text{......................... 4.2}$$

Where

N = nozzle flow (l/min)
A = application rate (l/ha)
W = nozzle spacing on boom or spray width (cm)
S= Speed (km/h)

$$S \ (m/s) = \frac{D \ (m) \ x \ 3.6}{t \ (s)} \quad \text{............... 4.3}$$

Where D = distance (m), t = (s)

Knowing the travel speed and maintaining a constant rate are crucial to good calibration and application. To reduce errors, it is advisable to check tachometer and throttle setting speeds by timing the travel over a measured distance. Perform this speed check in the field similar to the one to be sprayed, with the sprayer at least half full of water and using the throttle setting and gear that will be used for spraying.

3.7   Fruit harvesting technologies

Two technologies are popularly employed in fruits and vegetables harvest;

1. *Manual harvest technology by hand picking* and.
2. *Mechanical harvest technologies through* tree shaking or by the use of mechanical aids such as harvesting tools and machine harvesters.

3.7.1 Manual harvesting technologies

Manual harvest technology employed human labour in harvest, the use of mechanical aids give rise to the following advancements in machine technology. Manual harvesters should be well trained in the proper way to harvest the crop to minimize damage and waste, and should be able to recognize the proper maturity stage for the produce they are handling.

Manual harvesting practices

Harvesting practices should cause as little mechanical damage to produce as possible. Gentle digging, picking and handling will help reduce crop losses. Pick carefully to avoid damage:

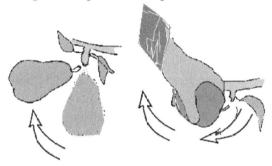

Figure 4-86: Picking fruits

For some crops, a natural break point forms at the junction of the stem and the stalk when produce is mature. Harvesters should grasp the product firmly but gently and pull upward as illustrated below. Wearing cotton gloves, trimming fingernails, and removing jewellery such as rings and bracelets can help reduce mechanical damage during harvest.

Figure 4-87: Plucking fruits

If a small amount of leafy vegetables are being harvested for home use or for sale at a nearby roadside or farmers' market, a small tub of cold water can be useful for cooling the produce. The tub can be brought directly to the field and used by the picker as a field container. Clean water should be used with each lot of produce. Chilling leafy vegetables by using cold water at harvest will help maintain quality and prevent wilting.

Figure 4-88: Harvesting vegetables

Manual harvesting tools

Some fruits need to be clipped or cut from the parent plant. Clippers or knives should be kept well sharpened. Peduncles, woody stems or spurs should be trimmed as close as possible to prevent fruit from damaging neighbouring fruits during transport. Majority of fruits and vegetables are harvested by hand using secateurs, clippers, knives or diggers. Some fruits such as citrus, grapes and mangoes, needed to be clipped or cut from the plant (Figure 2-12).

Figure 2-12: Harvesting with secateurs

Some manual harvest equipment and tools, description and uses have been described in section 2.2.5.

Using the equipment

Pickers should harvest with care, by snapping, cutting or pulling the fruit or vegetable from the plant in the least damaging manner. The tips of knives should be rounded to minimize inadvertent gouges and excess damage to perennial plants. Knives and clippers should always be well sharpened. Pickers should be trained to empty their picking bags and/or baskets with care, never dumping or throwing produce into field containers. If harvesters pick directly into large bulk bins, produce can be protected from bruising by the use of a deaccelerating chute fashioned from canvas. Vented, stackable field containers should be kept clean and smooth.

3.7.2 Mechanical harvesting technologies

The idea of a mechanized harvesting system was developed from the post harvest challenges faced by the agricultural industry due to the lack of labour availability. Also, horticultural products have been known to be highly perishable, so care is required when selecting harvest and handling method. The selection of a harvesting procedure will depend on the characteristics of the product.

Trunk shake catch harvest systems

The trunk shake catch frame harvest systems consisted of 2 self-propelled units (each with 1 operator) & operated in the 2-row bedded groves.

Figure 4-92: Trunk shaker/deflector fruit harvester

The shaker unit operated in the ditch middle with a deflector frame that diverted fruit to the receiver unit on the opposite side of the tree or row. The receiver unit operated in the middle on top of the bed & initially conveyed harvested fruit into 10 box containers, tubs or flexible containers.

Canopy area shake catch harvest systems

The machine had 4 rectangular shaped shaking heads with plastic probes. Fruit was removed when these probes were inserted into the canopy & each head was hydraulically driven in a circular motion to shake the canopy to ~ a 30 inch depth. The 4 heads were not dynamically balanced & were mounted on a boom with which the machine operator could position the heads successively in all areas of the canopy. The machine was developed to shake non-uniform & tall trees which were generally not suitable for other shake catch systems.

Figure 4-93: Canopy shake fruit harvester

Canopy penetrator

Canopy penetrator has a rectangular array of tubes with spring loaded fingers which were inserted into tree canopy and then withdrawn., after 1 & 2 insertions 67 to 91% of the fruits volume penetrated were removed the by the tubes.

Figure 4-94: Spring loaded hooks near outer end of tubes

Figure 4-95: Canopy penetrator pull harvest system (Crunkelton's prototype)

Continuous travel canopy shake & catch harvest systems

The continuous travel canopy shaker utilizes 2 oscillating spoke drums to removed 70 to 90% of the fruits in the portion of the canopy penetrated by the spokes. Another design of the continuous travel canopy shaker utilized a self-propelled double drum (each drum 12 foot diameter & 12 feet high) shaker with catch frame & opposite tree row side self propelled catchframe.

Figure 4-96: USDA continuous travel shaker

Because the double drum design made the shake catch machine quite long & difficult to maneuver at row ends, a single compact drum shaker with alternate sets of spokes in the drum which moves horizontally in opposite directions for dynamic balance and reliability.

Figure 4-97: Oxbo pull behind continuous canopy shaker

4.8   Horticultural processing machines

Fruit processing machines include complete plants required to process all types of fruits into juice, concentrate, jam and freshly prepared pieces, with packaging to suit. The followings are few examples of the fruit processing machine.

Manual fruit/grain sorting

Incoming produce is placed in the sorting bin, sorted by one worker into the packing bin, and finally packed. The surface of the portable sorting table in Figure 4-98 below is constructed from canvas and has a radius of about 1 meter (about 3 feet).

Figure 4-98: Sorting table (PHTRC, 1984)

The edges are lined with a thin layer of foam to protect produce from bruising during sorting, and the slope from the center toward the sorter is set at 10 degrees. Produce can be dumped onto the table from a harvesting container, then sorted by size, colour and/or grade, and packed directly into shipping containers. Up to 4 sorters/packers can work comfortably side by side.

Fruit grader

The fruit grader employs stepwise expanding pitch fruit grading mechanism based on the principle of changing the flap spacing along the length of movement of fruits. The grading mechanism has provision to separate fruits into grades. The grading mechanism consists of two tracks of conveyor chains, matching sprockets, stainless steel flaps, and conveyor supports, flap space adjusting mechanism, sidewalls and fruit collecting chutes.

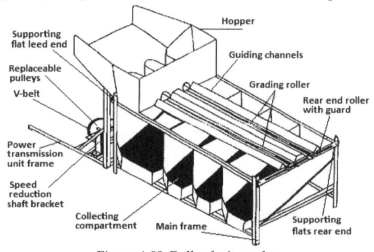

Figure 4-99: Roller fruit grader

The grader can be used to grapefruits such as apple, sweet lemon, oranges and larger size fruits. It is provided with elevator feeder for constant feeding of fruits in grading mechanism (Figure 4-100).

Figure 4-100: Fruit grading

The grader can be used to grapefruits such as apple, sweet lemon, oranges and larger size fruits. It is provided with elevator feeder for constant feeding of fruits in grading mechanism (Figure 4-101).

Figure 4-101: Weight sorter

Electronic colour sorter

The electronic colour sorter consists of a microprocessor-based roller feeding system provided with a three way scanning system which enables all round viewing of various grains, resulting in better quality of accepted and rejected product. The machine is equipped with hybrid signal conditioning, which allows ultra fast and reliable signal processing. It is independent of variations in light intensity and background because of the auto-annulling feature.

Figure 4-102: Fruit colour sorter

Manually operated coconut splitting machine

Coconut is the world's largest nut with varying size and shell thickness. A nutcracker (cocosplit) is mechanically used to split coconut with a firm blow from a large 1350 gram (3 pound) hammer. The juice can be saved by pre-draining, or by standing the cocosplit in a small bucket or plastic dish. A stout elastic band wrapped around the nut to avoid loss of juice and restrains the half nuts from "exploding" out of the dish (Figure 4-103).

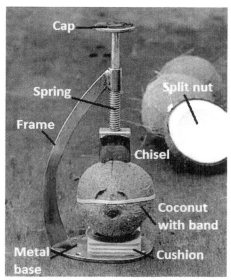

Figure 4-103: Cocosplit mechanism (Mike Foale, 2012)

The cocosplit mechanism consists of a base plate for saving the juice, a circular cap, chisel point and spring. Locate the nut carefully on the cushion of the base-plate. Direct contact between shell and the metal base-plate may cause a jagged break in the shell.

The manually operated splitting device is used for splitting dehusked coconuts. It consists of a pedestal, pivoted long handle, cutting knife and a platform Figure 4-90. Lifting the handle raises the knife. The dehusked nut is placed on the platform and then the knife is lowered to cut the nut. The coconut water is collected is a pot or container placed at the base of platform after splitting the nut.

Figure 4-104: Manually operated coconut splitting machine

Coconut punch & splitter

The manually operated splitting device is used for splitting dehusked coconuts. It consists of a pedestal, pivoted long handle, cutting knife and a platform. Lifting the handle raises the knife (Figure 4-105). The dehusked nut is placed on the platform and then the knife is lowered to cut the nut. The coconut water is collected is a pot or container placed at the base of platform after splitting the nut.

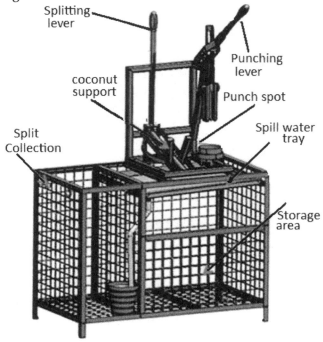

Figure 4-105: Manual punch and splitting machine, (IndiaMART, 2008)

Mechanical coconut dehusking

The traditional method of dehusking by farmers by using simple tools such as knife blade or spear is hampered by poor productivity. The need for mechanization is important for preparation of coconut in large-scale industrial processing due to labour shortages. In recent years, several machines were developed for dehusking of coconuts.

Figure 4-106: Mechanical coconut dehusking

This machine uses power from a 5-hp engine and transmits to it to a hydraulic pump. The Hydraulic pump transmitted the power to the double spiked rollers which have 33 spikes on each roller. Both rollers are set in parallel position with 45 degree from base frame. The two rollers will rotate in opposite direction and scrapped the coconut skin and split the husk and nuts. The position of the frame ensures easy dropping of the coconut by gravity at one side and husk is spitted at the other side automatically.

Soybean flaking machine

The flaking machine consists of three mild steel rollers (knurled and chromium plated surface), mainframe, hopper, stand, and collecting tray and drive mechanism. It is suitable for producing flakes from soybean, sorghum, maize and Bengal gram. It is driven by one hp single-phase electric motor through belt and pulleys and the drive to the rollers is by spur gears.

Soybean blanching unit

Blanching of soybean is carried out to remove anti-nutritional ingredients. It is essentially a water heater with the provision for inserting and removing the containers of soybean. It has a central cylinder through which the hot flue gases pass to heat the water, which is stored in a concentric outer cylinder Figure 4-107.

Figure 4-107: Soybean blanching unit

The outer cylinder is insulated with asbestos rope to conserve heat. Soybean is placed in stainless steel perforated cages and immersed in the hot water. It consists of central heating cylinder, outer cylinder, asbestos rope insulation, stainless steel.

Melon depodding machine

The mechanics of melon depodding include compression, shearing and impact. The main function of the melon-depodding machine is to break the melon pod and separate the seeds from the pod and the pulp.

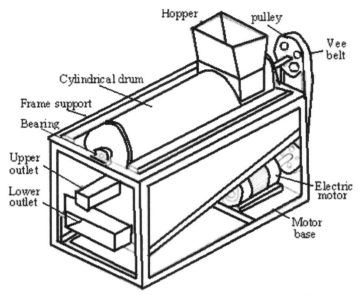

Figure 4-108: Melon depodding machine (Oloko and Agbetoye, 2006)

The hopper serves as the feeding mechanism through which the melon pod is fed into the machine. The spike, through their impact force breaks the pod and the melon seeds, are separated from the pod and are subsequently collected through the outlets. The screw conveyor containing spikes conveys both the depodded melon pulp and seeds into the discharge outlets (Figure 4-108).

Vegetable dryer

The vegetable dryer is specially designed for drying high moisture crops such as Cauliflower, Cabbage and Onion etc to a low level of moisture content. It consists of a drying chamber, plenum chamber, heating chamber a blower Figure 4-109.

Figure 4-109: Soybean blanching unit

The drying trays are made of aluminum and have nylon mesh is provided for keeping the produce. Temperature control is achieved with the help of the thermostat provided in the unit. Moisture content of the produce can be reduced from 90% to 6% in a batch of 50 kg in 11-14 hours.

4.9   Fruit quality measurement equipments

Quality is a complex criterion by which the acceptability and many attributes of foods are judged. Some of these quality attributes are: flavour, texture firmness, size shape and appearance. Objective evaluation of quality in fruits and vegetable is determined by using instruments. These instruments and their features are considered below.

Colorimeter

Minolta colorimeter is an instrument used to assign a specific colour value based on the amount of light reflected off the commodity surface or the light transmitted through the commodity. The Minolta Colorimeter can detect small differences in color and provides separate values for lightness to darkness, green to red and blue to yellow scales.

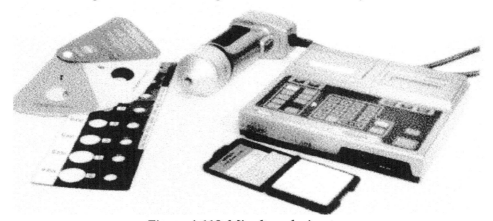

Figure 4-110: Minolta colorimeter

Advantages

a. Less variability in color measurement.
b. Can measure small differences in color accurately.
c. Can be automated on the packing line.
d. Portable hand-held units are available (Figure 4-110).

Disadvantages

a. Requires specialized equipment at a significant cost.
b. May be slower than subjective evaluation.

Penetrometer

The most common device used to assess firmness is the penetrometer. This has a cylindrical probe, the end of which is pushed into the object to be measured. The force required to give a predetermined penetration is recorded. In most fruit a section of the skin is removed first to expose the flesh.

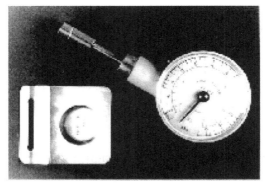

Figure 4-111: Effigi Penetrometer

The penetrometer then gives an index of the firmness of the product tissue. Several versions have been developed. The Magness Taylor penetrometer is forced into the tissue, compressing a spring. When the probe has penetrated to a specified depth, the reading is taken from the spring compression. An alternative, more compact version is the Effigi penetrometer, which has a coiled spring so that the force can be read off a dial (Figure 4-112).

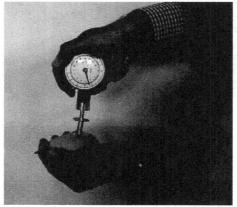

Figure 4-112: Using the penetrometer

Texture analyzers

Research laboratories commonly use universal testing machines to determine physical properties of crops. Sensitive universal testing machines have been developed that are dedicated to the measurement of food texture. Indenting heads include a penetrometer cylinder, a spherical indenter, and a flat plate to give compression tests between parallel platens. One system measures the bursting strength of the skin of tomatoes and the whole-fruit compression resistance in the same test. Measurements can be taken on whole fruits and vegetables or cut samples.

Twist tester

An alternative destructive tester has been developed in which the fruit is pushed onto a blade mounted on a spindle, so that the blade enters the fruit at a predetermined depth under the skin. The fruit is rotated, so that the blade turns at a fixed depth (Figure 4).

Figure 4-113: Twist tester

A rising weight on the end of an arm is used to apply an increasing moment (torque) to the blade, to resist the rotation. Eventually failure of the tissue occurs, and the moment can be calculated from the angle of the arm. It has been used successfully to measure the texture of apples, mangoes, plums, and other fruits.

Refractometer

The levels of soluble solids in fruit and vegetable juices can be determined by measuring the refractive index of the juices. Laboratory and field devices require a small sample of juice placed on a glass cover. The refraction of the light produces an indication on a scale that gives a measure of the soluble solids directly. This is a useful indicator of maturity at harvest time.

Figure 4-114: Refractometer

Description: Refractometers have features such as automatic temperature compensation, thumb screw for easy calibration, Brix measurement range (e.g., measurement between 0-32 percent with 0.2% accuracy) and padded casing. Refractometers are low in cost but may require calibration. Measurements may be affected by temperature and delays in carrying out the test after exposing fresh juice.

Uses: Handheld refractometer is used for measuring the amount of dissolved solids in fruits and vegetables. It is particularly useful for measuring sugar levels in grapes

Digital refractometers

Digital refractometers remove potential operator error in reading values.

For small products such as cherries, strawberries and grapes, the entire fruit can be juiced. For larger products, a sample wedge should be cut from stem to blossom end and to the center of the fruit to account for variability in SSC from top to bottom and inside to outside of the fruit. A garlic press works well for small samples. Cheese cloth may be necessary to remove pulp from the juice.

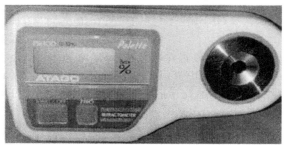

Figure 4-115: Digital refractometer

A wedge is cut from the commodity from stem to blossom end and to the center. The juice is extracted with a garlic press and a few drops are placed onto the glass of the refractometer. The refractometer is closed and held up to the light for viewing through the eyepiece. The internal scale will show the SSC of the juice.

4.10   Packing and packaging materials

Because it is possible to preserve food by altering their immediate environment, packaging has become an important element in preservation. Satisfactory packaging requires consideration of protection, economy, convenience and appearance. Factors affecting the choice of packaging materials include:

1. Product properties
2. Storage condition
3. Properties of economically available material.

The choice of packaging for fruits and vegetable is affected by

1. The tendency of food to gain or lose moisture,
2. Its free fat content,
3. Its particle size, tendency to sift and
4. Its susceptibility to spoilage by light, oxygen and organisms.

Field packing

When crops are field packed the picker harvests and then immediately packs the produce after minimal handling. A simple aid for field packers is a movable cart with a rack for boxes and a wide roof to provide shade. This cart is designed to be pushed by hand along the outer edge of the field or orchard where harvest is taking place. It has been used to field pack table grapes, small fruits and specialty vegetables. A self-propelled field pack system allows field workers to cut, trim, tie/wrap and pack in the field, thus eliminating the expense of operating a packing shed.

4.10.1 Packaging materials and requirements

Packaging material requirement

Packaging can be both an aid and a hindrance to obtaining maximum storage life and quality depending on handling practice. Packages need to be strong enough to prevent collapse. Packages should be designed to allow cool air to flow directly over products, ensuring rapid temperature pull-down and consequent temperature maintenance. Regrettably, too many packages in current use are largely impenetrable to air movement, resulting in a slow temperature decrease, influencing quality negatively.

Sacks

Sacks are commonly used to package produce, since they tend to be inexpensive and readily available. None of the types of sacks available are good for protecting fresh produce, and they should be avoided whenever possible.

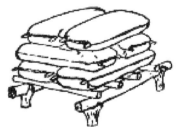

Figure 4-116: Pile of sacks on a pallet

These sacks are especially suitable for the dry tropics. Because of the danger of moisture uptake they should not be placed on concrete floors or on the ground, but on plastic sheets, waterproof canvas or on wooden pallets.

Fibreboard containers

The diagrams below are for a variety of commonly used fiberboard containers. Final dimensions can be altered to suit the needs of the handler, and all containers should have adequate vents. Cartons can be glued, taped or stapled as desired during construction at the packinghouse.

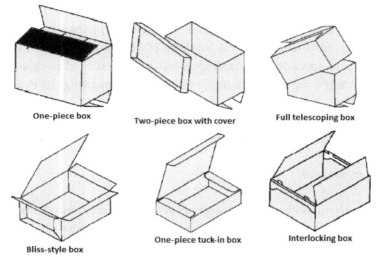

One-piece box   Two-piece box with cover   Full telescoping box

Bliss-style box   One-piece tuck-in box   Interlocking box

Figure 4-117: Fiberboard container designs

Waxed cartons, wooden crates and plastic containers:

If produce is packed for ease of handling, waxed cartons, wooden crates or rigid plastic containers are preferable to bags or open baskets, since bags and baskets provide no protection to the produce when stacked. These materials are reusable and cost effective when used for the domestic market and can also withstand high relative humidity found in the storage environment.

Figure 4-118: Carton with fiberboard divider

Hand-pack

Produce can be hand-packed to create an attractive pack, often using a fixed count of uniformly sized units. Packaging materials such as trays, cups, wraps, liners and pads may be added to help immobilize the produce. Simple mechanical packing systems often use the volume-fill method or tight-fill method, in which sorted produce is delivered into boxes, then vibration settled.

Figure 4-119: Sample of DRC with tomatoes

Figure 4-120: Sample of RPC with apples

Plastic films

Packaging in plastic films can modify the atmosphere surrounding the produce (modified atmosphere packaging or MAP). MAP generally restricts air movement, allowing the product's normal respiration processes to reduce oxygen content and increase carbon dioxide content of the air inside the package.

Pressure-pack trays

Once sorted into grades and size, fruit are delivered by conveyor to a packing area. Here fruit may be held in rotating final size bins until they can be packed by hand into cartons. Alternatively, if automatic tray fillers are used, fruit fall into a paper pulp tray directly. Fruit and vegetables also may be wrapped individually in foam liners or films before, or instead of, packing them in a rigid container.

Figure 4-121: Pressure-pack tray system

Internal and external failures of both rigid and flexible containers frequently reduce quality or spoilage life of products, resistance to moisture, corrosion, leakage and package fatigue are needed to withstand high temperature or humidity or the corrosive action of certain products high in salt, fat natural acid sulphur compounds.

Peg-type trays

Packaging fulfils several functions including containment, facilitating transportation, protection of fruit from further damage, protection of the environment from contents of package (for example, if the contents are dirty), marketing, product advertising, and stock control.

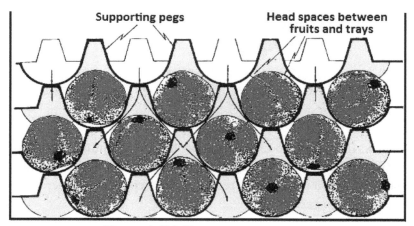

Figure 4-122: Peg-type tray system

Modified atmosphere packaging (MAP)

Modified atmosphere packaging is the process of matching commodity and film permeability characteristics to evolve an appropriate passively atmosphere through the consumption of O_2

and production of CO_2 during respiration (Kader, 2002). Some rigid plastic consumer packages are designed with a gas diffusion window through which a partial vacuum is created and a gas mixture of 30 to 50% O_2 and 4 to 6% CO_2 is introduced into the bag through gas diffusion window, which is then sealed. Fresh-cut or lightly processed lettuce (shredded or chopped) can be packaged in 5-mil plastic bags employing this treatment method and packaging.

Figure 4-123: Sealed plastic bag

Many plastic films are available for packaging, but very few have gas permeability that makes them suitable for MAP. Low density polyethylene and polyvinyl chloride are the main films used in packaging fresh fruits and vegetables. Polyesters have low gas permeability that they are suitable only for commodities with very low respiration rates.

Labelling

On the international market, some fresh fruits require considerable detail. This may include, for example, harvest date, packing date, and name of grower and packer, as well as details about the cultivar and grade. This information can be critical if quality management problems arise in the retail market.

Libelling packages helps handlers to keep track of the produce as it moves through the postharvest system, and assists wholesalers and retailers in using proper practices. Labels can be pre-printed on fibreboard boxes, or glued, stamped or stencilled on to containers. Brand labelling packages can aid in product packer, and producer advertisement. Some shippers also provide brochures detailing storage methods or recipes for consumers.

Labelling of consumer packages is mandatory under FDA regulations. Labels must contain the name of the product, net weight, and name and address of the producer, packer or distributor. Shipping labels contain some or all of the following information:
- Brand name.
- Common name of the product.
- Net weight, count and/or volume.
- Name and address of packer or shipper.

- Country or region of origin.
- Size and grade.
- Recommended storage temperature.
- Special handling instructions.
- Names of approved waxes and/or pesticides used on the product.

CHAPTER 5

MACHINERY HANDLING & EQUIPMENT SAFETY

Content: Introduction to tools and equipment preparation for field operation, hand tool and machine safety rules, horticultural tractor operation and safety, ATV safety and equipment sterilization

5.0 Introduction

Horticulture and landscape workers uses hand tools such as spade, fork etc and small-engine powered machines, such as push mowers, ride-on mowers, weed trimmers, and leaf blowers, in the course of executing their work. These tools and machinery uses mechanical power and thus have similar characteristic hazards with all agricultural, industrial and domestic machines. Today's horticultural machinery have become extremely specialized and designed to perform many different tasks.

While these mechanical systems save valuable time and are beneficial to horticultural productivity, they also present an ever-present danger to the people who operate them. The purpose of this chapter is to acquaint the students and workers with various possible hazards associated with tool handling and machinery moving parts, etc. and the need to protect employees from the hazards resulting from these machines.

5.1 Tools and equipment preparation

Preparing for work

In preparing for horticultural operations such as pruning, brushing, or weeding involving the use of hand tools, there is a need to ensure that a risk assessment be undertaken in order to get all workers acquainted with possible hazards and comply with identifiable control measures.

A safe method of operation for the work to be done must be agreed to ensure a safe working distance can be maintained between workers and any machinery (out of the risk zones of the tools or machinery being used).

Make sure a designated and responsible person knows the daily work programme and agree with them a suitable emergency procedure.

Causes of hand tool hazards

The following causes have been identified as possible causes of hand and tool hazards;

1. *Wrong usage of tool*: The greatest hazards posed by hand tools result from misuse and improper tool maintenance. Careless and/or lack of skillful use of tools such as files and rasps could cause numerous injuries. For instance a knife that slips can severe a nerve, tendon, or blood vessel.
2. *Unsafe practices*: Engaging tools in jobs and operations not intended or designed for could result in hazard.

General safety tips for tools and equipment use

The following safety rules applies generally to all tools and equipment while in operation

1. Always wear personal protection clothing such as safety goggles with shields, earmuffs or earplugs, leather or cotton gloves, long pants, and rubber-soled work boots or shoes. Do not wear tennis shoes, sandals, or open-toed shoes.
2. Remove any loose debris (trash, tree limbs, rocks, etc.) before you start.
3. Make sure the area where you will be working is clear of all other workers or bystanders, especially small children and pets. Check the operator's manual for proper clearance of flying debris.
4. Never operate a machine while under the influence of alcohol, drugs, or medication.
5. Never remove any safety guards or shields. They are there for your protection.

Safe use of cutters

Cutters used on stocks, scion etc should have enough capacity for the stock; otherwise, the jaws may be sprung or spread. Cutters require frequent lubrication. To keep cutting edges from becoming nicked or chipped, cutters are not to be used as nail pullers or pry bars. Cutter jaws should have the hardness specified by the manufacturer for the particular kind of material to be cut.

Safe use of edge cutting tool

Edged tools are to be used so that if a slip should occur, the direction of force will be away from the body. For efficient and safe work, edged tools are to be kept sharp and ground to the proper angle. A dull tool does a poor job and may stick or bind.

a. *Wood chisels*: Inexperienced employees shall be instructed in the proper method of holding and using chisels. Handles are to be free of splinters. The wood handle of a chisel struck by a mallet is to be protected by a metal or leather cap to prevent it from splitting. The work to be cut must be free of nails to avoid damage to the blade or cause a chip to fly into the user's face or eye.
b. *Saws*: Saws should be carefully selected for the work they are to do. For crosscut work on green wood, a coarse saw (4 to 5 points per inch) is to be used. A fine saw is better for smooth, accurate cutting in dry wood. Saws are to be kept sharp and well set to prevent binding.
c. *Axes:* An axe person is to make sure that there is a clear circle in which to swing the axe before starting to chop. Also, all vines, brush, and shrubbery within the range should be removed; especially overhead vines that may catch or deflect the axe. Axe blades shall be protected with a sheath or metal guard wherever possible. When the blade cannot be guarded, it is safer to carry the axe at one's side. The blade on a single edged axe shall be pointed down.
d. *Hatchets:* Hatchets shall not be used for striking hard metal surfaces since the tempered head may injure the user or others by flying chips. When using a hatchet in a crowded area, employee shall take special care to prevent injury to themselves and other workers. Using a hatchet to drive nails is prohibited.

Screwdrivers

The practice of using screwdrivers for punches, wedges, pinch bars, or pries shall not be allowed. Cross-slot (Phillips-head) screwdrivers are safer than the square bit type, because they have lesser tendency to slip. The tip must be kept clean and sharp, however, to permit a good grip on the head of the screw. The part to be worked upon must never be held in the hands; it should be laid on a bench or flat surface or held in a vise.

Figure 5-1: Screwdrivers

5.2 Hand tools and safety rules

Use of weeding and cleaning tools

The following safety rules applies when working with weed and cleaning tools

a. Make sure a firm stance is maintained and there is enough clear, unimpeded space to swing the cutting tool safely.
b. Do not swing the cutting tool directly towards the legs.
c. When using a short-handled hook, keep your free hand well away from the cutting direction. A forked stick may be used to keep the free hand away from the cutting tool.

Safe use of clippers and knives

Clippers or knives should be kept well sharpened and clean. Peduncles, woody stems or spurs should be trimmed as close as possible to prevent fruit from damaging neighboring fruits during transport. Care should be taken to harvest pears so that the spurs are not damaged. Pruning shears can be used for harvesting fruits and some vegetables.

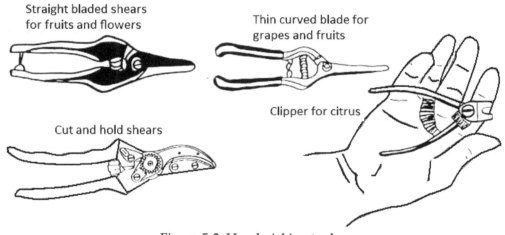

Straight bladed shears for fruits and flowers

Thin curved blade for grapes and fruits

Clipper for citrus

Cut and hold shears

Figure 5-2: Hand picking tools

Safe use of hand saws for brushing and pruning

The following safety rules applies when working with hand saws

a. Make sure you maintain a firm stance and there is enough clear, unimpeded space to use the saw safely.
b. Keep ditches clear of brash.
c. Be alert to hazards such as wasps' sting, wild life habitat etc.
d. Take extra care when working on broken ground, near drains etc.
e. Do not stand astride the saw handle.

f. Stand so you are clear of falling branches when pruning.

Do not carry out high pruning work if any part of the equipment or tree can come within 15 m of an energised overhead power line. Where pruning is within two tree lengths of an overhead power line, obtain further advice from the owner of the line.

5.3 Power tool safety rules

Safety checks in handling agricultural machinery

Accidents are most likely to happen when machinery operators are not in top physical or emotional condition or when they are tired, ill, worried, angry, or have their minds on something else. However, constant alertness is also necessary to prevent machinery accidents. The operator must be aware of hazards and remain alert to situations that are potentially dangerous. These hazards alertness include:

a. *Preoperational checks* on starting, operating, transporting, towing, field repair and maintenance of the machinery is required.
b. *Hand signals*: Since spoken instructions are very difficult to hear over the sounds of most machinery, knowledge of hand signals can be extremely helpful to the operator when manoeuvring especially in tight places.
c. *Safety before starting*: The more you know about the machinery, the better prepared you will be to safely operate it. If the machinery is run (operated) inside a building, make sure to open the doors to provide good ventilation. Always clean the machine before starting. Trash around exhaust system can cause fires, remove them. Oil, grease or mud on ladders or the platform can cause serious falls, so clean them with solvent. If the machinery is equipped with a cab, clean the glass to provide maximum visibility.
d. *Check the tyre pressure* each day. Under-inflation can cause buckling of the sidewall, which can cause dangerous tyre failure. Over-inflated tyres have a great deal of "bounce" and cause upsets more readily than tyres with correct pressure. Always use the handrails and ladders provided on the combine for safe mounting and dismounting.

a. The machinery maintenance factor

Machinery maintenance is another factor affecting the kevel of machine hazard. Poorly maintained machinery have high tendency of harbouring hazard due to frequent machinery breakdown. All equipment should be thoroughly cleaned with a high-pressure washer to remove dirt and trash residue. Accumulated trash and dirt can create fire hazards, electrical malfunctions, corrosion and rust of equipment, which may result in breakdowns.

Many operators follow a good cleanup with a wax job to help protect the equipment from corrosion, oxidation and major downtime. Once equipment is clean, farmers should thoroughly service and lubricate the machine.

5.4   Component and machinery requirement for maintenance

The following components of machinery and equipment are required at some level of maintenance to avoid them constituting hazard points.

a.   *Engine/power train components*: A well maintained engine system shut off potential dangers. These parts needed maintenance to avoid breakdown and failure which could lead to injury. The engine and power train components if not properly maintained could be a potential source of injury during operation. For instance, a poorly maintained belt/pulley could cause sudden freedom of machine components which tend to trigger increased engine speed or abrupt stoppage or shutting off of hydraulic systems.

Figure 5-2: Typical compression ignition engines

Harmful acid accumulation in oil pan can damage engine components over the long wet months. Farmers should pay particular attention to the condition of their crankcase oil during rain operations. Regularly service your engine and replace both oil and fuel filters.

Contaminants can cause extensive damage to hydraulic systems. Equipment owners should check their tractor or combine fuel tanks, as well as their farm's bulk tanks, for condensation. Always filter the fuel and keep it clean and fresh for operation.

b.   *Electrical components:* Frayed or broken wires must be replaced, repair broken gauges, lights and switches. On idle machines, the battery ground cable should be disconnected from the battery to avoid corrosive build-up and possible battery discharge.
c.   *Tillage tools and components:* As minimum tillage requiring chemical incorporation becomes more popular, tillage tools are growing larger and more sophisticated. These demands have led to the development of more sophisticated hydraulic systems.

For instance, today's tillage multi-wing folding units require several hydraulic cylinders to properly perform their tasks. Regular maintenance of these complex mechanisms is required to keep the equipment in good condition.

Figure 5-3: Multi-wing slurry injection tank

Thorough coating of all hydraulic cylinder rods with a protective lubricant is advised against rust. Rusted cylinder rods can quickly damage seals. Don't forget to check the shanks on field cultivators. Worn shank bushings or pins should be replaced.

d. *Planters/drills components:* Like other equipment, planters and drills should be cleaned of any build-up, especially the seed or fertilizer hoppers. Make sure all movable parts are free and not stuck due to chemical corrosion. Operators should check all moving parts for excessive wear.

Figure 5-4: A typical seeder/ planter

On air planters, the condition of the cut-off brush is very important and should be adjusted properly. Finally, lubricate all moving parts and inspect all chains and other drive mechanisms for excessive wear or misalignment.

b. *Harvesting equipment:* Combine headers require special storage care. It is suggested that a closely monitored inspection of the header units, for worn, bent or broken parts and replacing them as needed guarantee efficiency of operation and safety. Proper adjustment of belts and chains is critical to prolong wear.

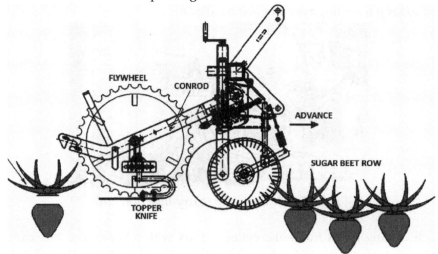

Figure 5-5: Sugar beet header

Operators should check all drives, auger, retractable fingers and stripper bars of the grain header etc for effective operation. Knife guards and other parts should be inspected for wear and replaced as needed. Round out the check up by lubricating and properly adjusting the grain header. Stalk roll knives should be sharpened or replaced and lubricated, and auger systems checked for proper function.

Remove the corn head check up by lubricating all main points including chains and other moving parts. Finally, equipment tyres should be cleaned and inspected for possible cuts. Check tyre pressures before storing equipment and inflate them as necessary.

c. *Seasonal machinery checks*: Off-season is the time to make those necessary repairs and adjustments to avoid undue downtime during the next busy season. During the busy early rainy season, electrical problems often are the most time-consuming to trace and repair. Dry season is a good time to check for loose connections, check for worn belts, loose bolts, oil leaks and the condition of all hoses, in addition to operational/ performance checks. Proper off-season machinery storage will add value to your farm equipment, increase its lifespan and decrease your operating costs. Before storing machinery unit, all soil engaging tools should be thoroughly cleaned and coated with a lubricant to guard against rust.

Rotary hand mower safety

Small rotary hand mowers are to be used in improving landscaped areas and in other areas that require mowing, but are inaccessible to tractor units. Traffic circles, intersection lawn areas, and steep slopes are such areas. Other locations to be mowed in this way include areas around culvert inlets and outlets, bridge ends, and immediate areas near highway signs, guardrails or posts, and traffic control devices.

There are precautions to be exercised when operating small rotary hand mowers. These precautions include clearing the area of debris before mowing, staying off wet slopes and locating of large rocks or similar objects to be avoided when mowing.

Other safety measures to be followed are those of disconnecting the ignition wire when cleaning or replacing blades, shutting off the engine when the mower is unattended or when refueling, and keeping fingers and feet away from rotary blades. Safety-toed shoes shall be worn when operating small hand rotaries. All shields and guards shall be in place when equipment is running.

Push mower safety

1. Start the mower from a firm stance with both feet in a safe position.
2. If the mower has a self-propelled mechanism, make sure it is disengaged before you start the engine. If the self-propelled mechanism is in gear, the mower will start to move once the engine has started.
3. Never use an electric mower in wet grass. You could receive an electrical shock.
4. Never perform any kind of adjustment while the mower is running. For example, if you want to change the height of the wheels, first turn the engine off and disconnect the spark plug. Then reposition the wheels.

Figure 5-6: Check the mower for debris, rock and other objects

5. Check the mower for debris, rock and other objects before mowing the lawn. Objects hit by the mower blade and thrown out from under the mower could result in severe injuries and deaths.

6. If the mower deck should become clogged with grass, stop the mower and turn the engine off before clearing the clog. Never touch any part of the mower while operating it except for the handles and throttles.

Figure 5-7: Danger sign for sharp knife

7. Always push the mower in a forward direction. Never pull the mower toward you. If you slip, your foot could go under the mower deck resulting in a serious injury.

8. If the lawn slopes. Mow across the slope with the walk-behind rotary mower, never mow up or down with a riding mower, drive up and down the slope, not across.

Figure 5-8: Mowing on the slope

Slopes that are 3:1 or steeper should not be mowed.

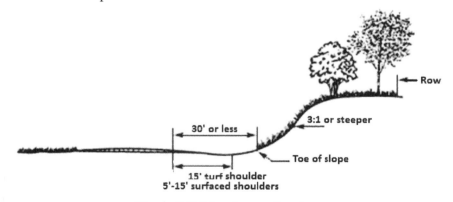

Figure 5-9: Mowing on the slope

Slopes that are flatter than 3:1, either cut or fill shall be mowed as shown in this diagram except when the entire right-of-way is mowed.

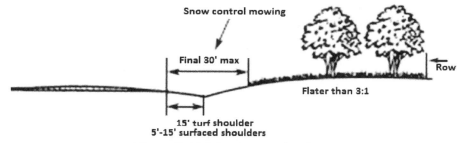

Figure 5-10: Mowing on the slope

The toe of the slope is the limit of mowing, even if it falls inside the 15-foot or snow control limits.

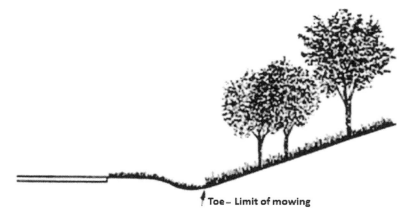

Figure 5-11: Mowing on the slope

9. If the mower has an attached grass catcher, stop the engine before detaching the grass catcher. Do not let the grass catcher become too full. A full or over-full catcher adds wear and tear on the engine and the mower does not cut as well.
10. Perform a safety check before and after each time you use the mower. Check and tighten all loose nuts, bolts, and screws. If the mower has a drive belt, check for frayed or worn sections. Replace the belt if necessary.
11. Clean the mower after each use including the underside of the mower deck. Clean the grass catcher, if the mower has one.

Walk-behind and ride-on mowers

While homeowners generally use walk-behind power lawnmowers to cut small plots of grass, many residents with large lawns have come to rely on riding mowers, lawn tractors, and garden tractors as indispensable machines for maintaining the landscape.

Hazards most often associated with riding equipment are blade contact and loss of stability. Fatal incidents have several common patterns: the machine tips over, the victim falls under or is run over by the machine (incidents involving young children are in this category), or the victim is thrown from or falls off the machine.

The voluntary safety standard for walk-behind and ride-on mowers is ANSI/OPEI B71.1-2003. If you are shopping for a new mower, a label certifying that the mower or garden tractor meets the 2003 ANSI B71.1 standard indicates that the machine has these safety features.

1. Operator presence control: This safety device will stop the rotary blades if the operator leaves the control position of the riding mower without first disengaging the blade drive. This feature will reduce the chance of injury if the operator leaves the control position to perform some other activity without first stopping the mower blade(s)
2. Increased seatback height: Look for seatbacks of at least 4 1/2 inches to help the operator maintain a safe position on the machine.
3. Dynamic turn and sudden traction performance limits have been added to improve machine stability.

In 2003 a requirement was added that prevents the mower from backing up with powered blades. This feature can reduce the severity of injuries that are caused when an operator backs into a young child by stopping the rotating blades.

Safe operating practices for ride-on mowers

This cutting machine is capable of amputating hands and feet and throwing objects. Failure to observe the following safety instructions could result in serious injury or death to the operator and/or bystander.

Read, understand, and follow all instructions on the machine and in the manual(s) before starting.

1. Clear the area of objects such as rocks, wire, toys, etc., which the blade(s) could throw.
2. Never carry passengers.
3. Stop the blades(s) when crossing gravel surfaces.
4. Do not operate machine without the entire grass catcher, discharge guard, or other safety devices in place and working.
5. Do not operate the machine while under the influence of alcohol or drugs.
6. Watch for traffic when operating near or crossing roadways.
7. Use extra care when loading or unloading the machine into a trailer or truck.
8. Always wear eye protection when operating machine.

DO NOT CARRY PASSENGERS

Figure 5-12: Passenger safety sign on ride-on mower

Slope operation

Slopes are a major factor related to loss of control and tip-over accidents, which can result in severe injury or death. Operation on all slopes requires extra caution.

MOW UP AND DOWN SLOPES   **DO NOT MOW ACROSS SLOPES**

Figure 5-13: Riding mower on the slope

1. Mow up and down slopes, not across.
2. Watch for holes, ruts, bumps, rocks, or other hidden objects. Uneven terrain could overturn the machine. Tall grass can hide obstacles.
3. Choose a low ground speed so you will not have to stop or shift while on a slope.
4. Do not mow on wet grass. Tires may lose traction.
5. Always keep the machine in gear when going down slopes. Do not shift to neutral and coast downhill.
6. Avoid starting, stopping, or turning on a slope.
7. Keep all movement on slopes slow and gradual. Do not make sudden changes in speed or direction, which could cause the machine to roll over.
8. Use extra care while operating the machine with grass catchers or other attachments; they can affect the stability of the machine. Do not use on steep slopes.
9. Do not try to stabilize the machine by putting your foot on the ground.

10. Do not mow near drop-offs, ditches or embankments. The machine could suddenly roll over if a wheel goes over the edge or if the edge caves in.

Weed trimmer safety

1. Keep your hands, face, and feet away from any moving parts. Do not touch the trimmer string while it is rotating.
2. If the trimmer should become entangled, stop the engine immediately. Then untangle the trimmer line.
3. Check for damage before restarting the engine.
4. Do not overreach. Always be properly balanced. Be alert if the area you are trimming is wet or on a slope.
5. Perform a safety check before and after each time you use the trimmer. Check and tighten all loose nuts, bolts, and screws.
6. Clean the trimmer after each use.

Leaf blower safety

1. Keep your hands, face, and feet away from any moving parts.
2. If your working area is dusty, wear a dust mask.
3. Do not overreach. Always be properly balanced. Be alert if the area you are trimming is wet or on a slope. Use caution while working on steps.
4. Never operate an electric blower if the area is wet.
5. Make sure the air intake is always free of debris.
6. Perform a safety check before and after each time you use the blower. Check and tighten all loose nuts, bolts, and screws.
7. Clean the blower after each use.

Chipper machine

Chipper machines cut tree limbs into small chips. Hazards arise when workers get too close to, or make contact with, the chipper. Contact with chipper operating components (blades, discs or knives) may result in amputation or death. Workers may also be injured by material thrown from the machine. To minimize these hazards, use appropriate engineering and work practice controls, including worker training.

Hazards

- Workers making contact with or being pulled into the chipper.
- Hearing loss.
- Face, eye, head or hand injuries.

Figure 5-14: Wood chipper (Courtesy: Bello, 2011)

- Never reach into a chipper while it is operating.
- Do not wear loose-fitting clothing around a chipper.
- Always follow the manufacturer's guidelines and safety instructions.
- Wear a hardhat, sturdy slip-resistant footwear, eye protection, hearing protection, and close fitting clothing (e.g. gloves without cuffs, pants without cuffs, shirtsleeves buttoned and shirts tucked in) when working with this equipment.

Figure 5-15: Chipper safe operation, EHS, 2004

- Feed brush and limbs butt-end first into the in-feed hopper.
- Walk away once the feed mechanism has grabbed the material.
- Workers should be trained on the safe operation of chipper machines. Always supervise new workers using a chipper to ensure that they work safely and never endanger themselves or others.
- Protect yourself from contacting operating chipper components.

- Prevent detached trailer chippers from rolling or sliding on slopes by chocking the trailer wheels.
- Maintain a safe distance (i.e., two tree or log lengths) between chipper operations and other work/workers.
- When servicing and/or maintaining chipping equipment use a lockout system to ensure that the equipment is de-energized.

Chain/power saw

The chain saw is a time saving and efficient power tool. It can be dangerous, however, causing injury or death in the hands of an uninformed and unaware operator. It is not the chain saw causing the accidents or injuries but the environment in which it is used.

Figure 5-16: Chainsaw, HSE, 2006

Safety features

Make sure that your chain saw has these features, and that the features are working:

1. Chain brake (manual or inertia)
2. Kickback guard
3. Chain catcher
4. Working safety throttle switch
5. Working on/off switch
6. Spark arrester

Personal protective wears

If you are going to help clear tree and wood debris, you should wear at least:

1. A helmet system (consisting of head, face and hearing protection)
2. Cotton or leather gloves
3. Chain saw protective chaps or chain saw protective pants (UL Listed)
4. A pair of chain saw protective work boots with steel toes

Safety tips in handling saw

1. Make sure your chain saw carburetor is properly adjusted. A trained servicing dealer should do this. A misadjusted carburetor will cause stalling or poor performance and could cause the operator to be injured.
2. If the saw is out of fuel, let it cool 30 minutes before refueling. Do not smoke when refueling the saw! Use a chain saw outdoors only.
3. Carry the chain saw with the engine off.
4. When bucking up (cutting) a downed tree, place a plastic wedge into the cut to keep your chain saw from binding up. They are available at any chain saw dealer and sometimes come packaged with the saw.
5. Never cut when tired or alone. Most woodcutting accidents occur late in the afternoon when most people are pushing to finish up for the day. Always work with a partner but never around children or pets.
6. Use a chain saw from the ground level only, not on a ladder or in a tree.
7. When felling a tree, keep everyone at least "two tree lengths away."
8. You should have a preplanned escape route.
9. It should be at a 45° angle from the projected direction of a falling tree. Make sure there is nothing that could trip or stop you from making a quick retreat.
10. When picking up heavy wood debris, get several helpers. Bend your knees and lift with your legs, not your back.

Tree felling using chainsaws

Before felling starts on the worksite:

1. Contact the owners of any overhead power lines within a distance equal to twice the height of any tree to be felled to discuss whether the lines need to be lowered or made dead;
2. Do not start work until agreement has been reached on the precautions to be taken;
3. Check whether there are underground services such as power cables or gas pipes which could be damaged when the tree strikes the ground;
4. If there are roads or public rights of way within a distance equal to twice the height of the tree to be felled, ensure that road users and members of the public do not enter the danger zone. You may need to arrange warning notices, diversions or traffic control.

When felling a tree:

- Check if it is affected by rot;
- assess what could affect the direction of fall, such as wind conditions and whether the tree is leaning, has uneven growth or branches which could foul other trees;

- Be especially careful to check for broken crowns and branches which might fall during the operation;
- Check both the tree to be felled and those nearby;
- operators may need to use aid tools such as alloy or plastic wedges, a breaking bar, a cant hook, a winch, or high-lift wedges and a sledgehammer;
- Make sure operators have the right equipment available and the skills to use it correctly.
- If a tree is likely to become hung-up on another during felling, operators will need to have the knowledge and the equipment to bring the hung-up tree down safely.

Dealing with leaning trees or wind-blown trees also requires special skills.

Working with chainsaws off the ground

Chainsaws should not be used off the ground unless the operator has been adequately trained in safe working techniques. Work off the ground involving the lifting and lowering of people or loads, including work-positioning techniques, will be subject to the requirements of the Lifting Operations and Lifting Equipment Regulations 1998 (LOLER).

Mobile elevating work platforms

Always use a purpose-built platform. Ensure operators have received adequate training in the safe operation of the platform and safe use of a chainsaw from a work platform.

Work from ladders

Avoid using a chainsaw from a ladder. Chainsaws require both hands to be operated safely: work on a ladder requires one hand to hold the ladder to maintain a steady working position. Work from a ladder should only be done by an arborist trained in and equipped for tree climbing. When operating from a ladder, the climber must establish an independent anchor to the tree using a rope and harness and obtain a stable and secure work position.

Ropes and harnesses

Using a chainsaw from a rope and harness requires special skills. This should only be done by people who have obtained the relevant competence certificate for arboricultural work.

Risks and hazards associated with chain saw

1. Hazards include broken or hanging branches, attached vines, or a dead tree that is leaning.
   a. If you have to cut a dead tree, be very careful! The top could break off and kill you.

b. If the tree is broken and is under pressure, make sure you know which way the pressure is going. If you're not sure, make small cuts to release some of the pressure before cutting up the section.

c. Be careful of young trees that other trees have fallen on. They act like spring poles and may propel the chain saw back into your leg. (Many professional loggers have been hurt in this manner.).

d. A downed tree may weigh several tons and can easily injure or kill an unaware chain saw operator.

e. More injuries occur during clean up after a hurricane than during the storm.

2. Kickback injury: To reduce the risk of kickback injury:

   a. Use a reduced kickback bar, low kickback chain and chain brake
   b. Avoid contact between the bar tip and any object
   c. Hold the chain saw firmly with both hands
   d. Do not over-reach
   e. Do not cut above shoulder height
   f. Check the chain brake frequently
   g. Follow sharpening and maintenance instructions for the chain saw.

Accident /incident alert case: unsafe tree-felling

New Zealand Department of labour on accident/incident alert No. 17, September 2006 reported a case of unsafe tree-felling leadings to death

Case: A firewood operator was killed when he was hit by a falling tree that had been poorly scarfed and back-cut. He had been felling trees on his own. He had placed an oversized scarf (60% of the tree's diameter) into the tree causing the tree to lean backward as he made the backcut, jamming the chainsaw. As he walked forward of the scarfed and back-cut tree to get his tools to remove the motor unit of his chainsaw the tree released and hit him from behind.

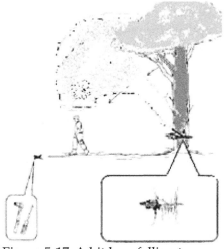

Figure 5-17: A hit by a falling tree

5.5 Horticultural tractor safety rules

Responsibility of personnel involved in mowing with tractors

Operator: There are numerous hazards to which the mower operator is subjected. These include: Washouts, ruts, culverts, markers, mowing on steep slopes, flying debris, passing motor vehicles, excessive operating speeds and others.

Employee: For the protection of employees, the supervisor shall inspect and patrol the area to be mowed for physical hazards. The supervisor shall also make sure that all personnel are fully clothed and are wearing bright orange or yellow-green clothing such as vests, shirts, jackets, coveralls and caps. Eye protection may also be required. For the added protection of employees, slopes that are 3:1 or steeper, or abnormal terrain where conditions are adverse, shall not be mowed. Sickle bar mowers shall be used with the sickle bar pointed toward the upside of the slope. The operator shall wear a safety seat belt when tractors are equipped with a Roll-Over Protection Structure (ROPS).

Children: Tragic accidents can occur if the operator is not alert to the presence of children. Children are often attracted to the machine and the mowing activity. *Never* assume that children will remain where you last saw them.

1. Keep small children out of the mowing area, and in the watchful care of a responsible adult other than the operator.
2. Be alert and turn machine off if a child enters the area.
3. Before and while backing, look behind and down for small children.
    4. Never carry children, even with the blade(s) shut off. They may fall off and be seriously injured or interfere with safe mower operation. Children who have been given rides in the past may suddenly appear in the mowing area for another ride and be run over or backed over by the machine.
5. Never allow children to operate the machine.
6. Use extreme care when approaching blind corners, shrubs, and trees, or other objects that may block your view of a child.

Safety during operation

Mowing side by side or in close tandem should be avoided. Stay far enough from each other to avoid any flying objects such as stones or other foreign materials. Stay in your seat until the power take-off has been disengaged and the mower has come to a complete stop. Never attempt to unclog or adjust a running machine even at idle speed. In raising a cutter bar, keep hands and fingers away from guards. Fingers can be severed by a falling knife even if the PTO is disengaged. Spare sickle bar blades shall be stored in such a manner that if the front of the tractor strikes an object, the spare blades cannot move into the operator's area. Mow with flow of traffic except in special circumstances or where permission is granted by your supervisor.

Safety while towing

1. Tow only with a machine that has a hitch designed for towing. Do not attach towed equipment except at the hitch point.
2. Follow the manufacturer's recommendation for weight limits for towed equipment and towing on slopes.
3. Never allow children or others in or on towed equipment.
4. On slopes, the weight of the towed equipment may cause loss of traction and loss of control.
5. Travel slowly and allow extra distance to stop.

Safety in general service

1. Never operate machine in a closed area.
2. Keep all nuts and bolts tight to be sure the equipment is in safe working condition.
3. If you strike a foreign object, stop and inspect the machine. Repair, if necessary, before restarting.
4. Never make any adjustments or repairs with the engine running.
5. Mower blades are sharp. Wrap the blade or wear gloves, and use extra caution when servicing them.
6. Check brake operation frequently. Adjust and service as required.
7. Maintain or replace safety and instruction labels, as necessary.

Safe handling of gasoline

To avoid personal injury or property damage, use extreme care in handling gasoline. Gasoline is extremely flammable and the vapour is explosive.

1. Extinguish all cigarettes, cigars, pipes, and other sources of ignition.
2. Use only an approved gasoline container.
3. Never remove gas cap or add fuel with the engine running. Allow engine to cool before refueling.
4. Never fuel the machine indoors.
5. Never store the machine or fuel container where there is an open flame, spark, or pilot light such as on a water heater or other appliances.
6. Never fill containers inside a vehicle or on a truck or trailer bed with a plastic liner.
7. Remove gas-powered equipment from the truck or trailer and refuel it on the ground. If this is not possible, then refuel such equipment with a portable container, rather than from a gasoline dispenser nozzle.

8. Keep the nozzle in contact with the rim of the fuel tank or container opening at all times until the fueling is complete. Do not use a nozzle lock-open device.
9. If fuel is spilled on clothing, change clothing immediately.
10. Never overfill fuel tank. Replace gas cap and tighten securely.

5.6   2-wheel tractor safety

A number of reports have highlighted safety issues associated with the operation of two-wheel tractors. The most common accidents involve crossing the bunds and road transport. The operation of two-wheel tractors for transport at night is a recognized hazard particularly as single headlights can be mistaken for a motorcycle. Research undertaken in Cambodia and Laos concluded that two-wheel tractors are involved in around five per cent of fatal accidents (Ericson and Matthew 2010). Occupational health and safety reports have recommended regular breaks for the machine operator due to vibrations. However, safety researchers have concluded that the risk to public safety must be weighed against the economic and social benefits (Ericson and Matthew 2010).

5.7   All terrain vehicles' safety rules

ATVs risk factors

There is a growing concern worldwide over the number of deaths and serious injury occurring in association with ATV operation in the context of agricultural as well as horticultural and pleasure uses of the machine. Known risk factors associated with ATV leading to deaths and serious injuries on farms include;

1. Human and behavioural factors,
2. Machine factors, and
3. Environmental factors.

Most Ag bike injuries result from lack of training and experience, speed, uneven or unfamiliar terrain, logs, rocks, embankments, carrying a passenger or an unbalanced load, inadequate protective clothing and unsafe driving. Those aged between 10 and 24 have a significantly higher risk of injury on ATVs. The following suggestions will help minimize risks.

a. Never ride an Ag bike without an approved helmet.
b. Long sleeves and pants, sturdy boots and gloves provide protection if you come off the vehicle.
c. Eye protection prevents serious eye injuries from bugs, branches or stones.

Maintenance safety

a. Check your bike before riding it.
b. Pay attention to maintenance advice in the vehicle manual.
c. Check brakes and tyres regularly.
d. Ensure all parts are genuine or are at least equivalent components designed for use on your particular brand of bike.

When operating a bike on road

a. Be on the lookout for potential hazards when riding. Rocks, bumps, irrigation pipes and wildlife all have the potential to cause an accident, and should be approached with caution.
b. Take extra care when operating a bike on unfamiliar or rough terrain. Where possible, use familiar farm tracks.
c. Avoid side overturns: Understand principles of center of gravity and centrifugal force.
d. Avoid high speeds and jerky steering and be aware of rough terrain.

Figure 5-18: Operator overran by an ATV

e. Be particularly careful when turning, approaching a rise or navigating an obstacle. If you are not sure of your ability to clear an obstacle, find another route or go back.
f. Don't drive ATVs on paved or bitumen surfaces. They are not intended for use on smooth surfaces and could be difficult to control.
g. Never ride ATVs on public roads. It may be difficult to avoid a collision if other vehicles are on the road.

5.8 Gardening tools and equipment sterilization

Gardening and horticultural tools are often used to remove diseased, rotting or dead foliage and plants. During this process, harmful bacteria are transferred to the gardening tools and should be removed so as to prevent the transfer of bacteria to healthy plants in the garden. By disinfecting gardening tools on a regular basis, you help prevent the spread of plant diseases in the garden. The following tips are employed to disinfect gardening tools.

1. *Remove dirt and debris from tools.* Before disinfecting tools, remove dirt, debris and sap by wiping the tools with a damp cloth or paper towels. The tools should be free of dirt and debris so the disinfecting solution can penetrate every cutting surface.
2. *Dip or soak tools in a disinfectant solution.* Many products can be used to disinfect gardening tools. Most products include basic household cleaning agents; however, commercially mixed gardening tool disinfectants are available at most garden centers. The amount of time necessary to dip or soak the tools varies depending on the disinfectant solution.

- Choose a bleach solution to disinfect gardening tools. Mix 1 gallon (3.8 liters) of water with 2 cups (.5 liters) of bleach in a bucket. Soak the tools in the bleach solution for about 10 minutes. Bleach solutions are highly effective in eliminating plant disease, but may corrode gardening tools with repeated use. Always wear protective masks and rubber gloves when cleaning tools with bleach solutions. Rinse tools immediately after soaking to avoid transfer of bleach to garden plants.
- Use ethanol or isopropyl alcohol to disinfect tools. Ensure that the alcohol is at least 70 percent pure for effective disinfecting. Fill a bucket with enough alcohol to cover a single tool. Soak 1 tool at a time for about 1 minute each. If you prefer, you may wipe tools with the alcohol rather than soaking them. Do not rinse the tools after disinfecting. Alcohol is flammable, so keep it away from open flames.
- Use detergent to clean gardening tools. A household detergent, like dishwasher detergent or laundry detergent, will remove viruses from garden tools. Mix about 1 cup (.2 liters) of detergent with 1 gallon (3.8 liters) of water. Soak the tools in the detergent mixture for several minutes. Rinse with water after disinfecting.
- Use Pine Sol to clean gardening tools. Fill a bucket with enough full-strength Pine Sol to cover a gardening tool. Soak the tool for 1 or 2 minutes. Pine Sol may be corrosive to gardening tools. Rinse with water after disinfecting to remove Pine Sol residue and keep the tools from corroding.
- Choose a Lysol solution to disinfect tools. Fill a bucket with about 20 percent liquid Lysol and 80 percent water. Soak the tools in the Lysol solution for several minutes. Of the general household products used to disinfect gardening tools, Lysol is the least corrosive. Lysol poses little threat to garden plants, so you do not need to rinse tools after application.
- Consider quaternary ammonium salts to clean tools. An effective disinfectant, quaternary ammonium salts are available through horticulture supply retailers or garden centers. Follow the directions on the product label. In most cases, the salts are mixed with water to create a cleaning solution. Hard water or organic matter may reduce the effectiveness of quaternary ammonium salts. Rinse tools after disinfecting.
- Select hydrogen dioxides to clean garden tools. Hydrogen dioxide, often referred to as oxygenated water, is less toxic than many other cleaning agents, but removes a limited number of pathogens from garden tools. Commercial hydrogen dioxide products are available from garden centers and horticulture supply retailers. To use hydrogen dioxides to clean gardening tools, follow the label instructions. Hydrogen dioxides may

corrode garden tools with repeated uses, so be sure to rinse tools thoroughly after application.

- Consider environmentally-friendly products like Physan 20 or Oxidate. Physan 20 is a broad-spectrum fungicide, while Oxidate is a hydrogen dioxide-based product that kills bacteria, algae and fungus on contact. These products are more expensive than most household cleaning products, and are available at select garden centers and commercial agriculture retailers. Follow label instructions for information on how to apply Physan 20 or Oxidate to disinfect gardening tools.

3. *Dry tools.* After disinfecting the gardening tools, dry them with a soft cloth. Do not allow water-based cleaning solutions to dry on the tools as they may rust the implements. In the case of pruning shears and other hinged tools, be sure to dry the inside and outside blades of the tool

BIBLOGRAPHY

List of references for further reading

ABM Garden Tools, 79A, Pocket GG-1, Vikas Puri, New Delhi – 110018, India. Website : www.abmtools.com : www.abmtools.net

AGGO, 2012. MF Grounds Care Equipment. A Range of Residential & Commercial

Agri-Fab 38-Inch Tow Lawn Sweeper. bestlawnsweeper.com/agri-fab-38-inch-tow-lawn-sweeper/

Ashby, B.H., et al., 1987. Protecting Perishable Foods During Transport by Truck. USDA, Office of Transportation, Agricultural Handbook Number 669.

Acland, J. D. 1971. *East African Crops*. London: United Nations Food and Agriculture Organization/Longman.

Amos, N. D., L. U. Opara, B. Ponter,C. J. Studman, and G. L.Wall. 1994. Techniques to assist with meeting international standards for the export of fresh produce from less developed countries. Proc. X11 CIGR World Congress, Milan, Italy, vol 2, pp. 1587–1594.

Bello R. S. (2007). Fundamental Principles of Agricultural Engineering Practice. Pub. Climax Printers #26/30 College Rd. Ogui New Layout, Enugu. ISBN: 978-080-015-8.

Bello R. S. (2006). Guide to Agricultural Machinery Maintenance, and Operation Pub; Fasmen Communications 79/94 Owerri Road, Okigwe Nigeria. ISBN: 978 - 2986 - 90 – 9).

Bello R. S. and Onilude M. A., (2011). Force Relations and Dynamics of Cutting Knife in a Vertical Disc Mobile Wood Chipper. *Leonardo electronic journal of practices and technologies issue 18*, January-June 2011 ISSN 1583-1078 p. 17-36 URL: http://lejpt.academicdirect.org/A18/017_034.htm

Bello R. S. Segun R. Bello, and Yahaya Mijinyawa, 2010. Assessment of Injuries in Small Scale Sawmill Industry of South Western Nigeria. Agricultural Engineering International: the CIGR Journal of Scientific Research and Development. Manuscript 1558. Vol. XII, March, 2010. URL:
http//:www.cigrjournal.org/index.php/Ejounral/article/view/1558/1293

Segun R. Bello and Femi Okelola, 2009. Assessment of work environment in small scale rice mills: a case study of Ivo LGA, Ebonyi State. *Proc. Of the 2nd international conference/workshop of the nigerian institution of agricultural engineers* South East Regional Chapter. Pp 36

Segun R. Bello, Adegbulugbe T. A. and Odey S. O., 2010. Farm Power and Machinery Operations, Repairs and Maintenance. ISBN: 978-3322254-4-3 Pub. Climax Printers #26/30 College Rd., Enugu Nigeria.

Bencini, M. C., and J. P. Walston. 1991. Post-harvest and processing technologies of African staple foods: A technical compendium. Agricultural Services Bulletin 89. Rome: United Nations Food and Agriculture Organization.

Beth Mitcham, Marita Cantwell, and Adel Kader,(2003). Methods for Determining Quality of Fresh Commodities. Perishables Handling Newsletter Issue No. 85 February 1996, Updated 6/16/03

Bodholt, O., 1985. Construction of cribs for drying and storage of maize. Agricultural Services Bulletin 66. Rome: United Nations Food and Agriculture Organization.

Cruz, J. F., and A. Diop., 1989. Agricultural engineering in development: Warehouse technique. Agricultural Services Bulletin 74. Rome: United Nations Food and Agriculture Organization.

Dauthy, M. E., 1995. Fruit and vegetable processing. Agricultural Services Bulletin 119. Rome: United Nations Food and Agriculture Organization.

De Lucia, M., and D. Assennato. 1994. Agricultural engineering in development: Post-harvest operations and management of food grains. Agricultural Services Bulletin 93. Rome: United Nations Food and Agriculture Organization.

Dhamija, O. P., and W. C. K. Hammer. 1990. Manual of food quality control: Food for export. Food and Nutrition Paper 14/6, Rev. 1. Rome: United Nations Food and Agriculture Organization.

Dixie, G. 1989. Horticultural marketing: A resource and training manual for extension officers. Agricultural Services Bulletin 76. Rome: United Nations Food and Agriculture Organization.

Eckman Wheeled Garden Leaf Vacuum, Blower & Shredder. www.mysmartbuy.com/p-886-Eckman-Wheeled-Garden-Leaf-Vacuum,-Blower-AND-Shredder.html

Enzafruit. 1996. New Zealand apple quality standards manual. Hastings, New Zealand: New Zealand Apple and Pear Marketing Board (Enzafruit International).

FAO. 1984. Manuals of food quality control: Food inspection. Food and Nutrition Paper 14/5. Rome: United Nations Food and Agriculture Organization.

FAO. 1993. Manual of food quality control: Quality assurance in the food control chemical laboratory. Food and Nutrition Paper 14/14. Rome: United Nations Food and Agriculture Organization.

FAO., 1995. Commodity review and outlook 1994–5. Economic and Social Development series 53. Rome: United Nations Food and Agriculture Organization.

FAO., 1985. Commodity review and outlook 1984–5. Economic and Social Development series. Rome: United Nations Food and Agriculture Organization.

FAO., 1986. *Improvement of Post-harvest Fresh Fruits and Vegetables Handling.* Bangkok: United Nations Food and Agriculture Organization.

FAO., 1989. Utilization of Tropical Foods. Food And Nutrition Bulletin 47 (No. 1 cereals, 2 roots and tubers, 3 trees, 4 beans, 5 oil seeds, 6 spices, 7 fruit, 8 animal products). Rome: United Nations Food and Agriculture Organization.

FAO., 1989. Quality control in fruit and vegetable processing. Food And Nutrition Bulletin 39. Rome: United Nations Food and Agriculture Organization.

Farm Electric Centre. 1989. *Grain Drying, Conditioning and Storage.* Stoneleigh, UK: Electricity Council, Farm Electric Centre.

Grierson, W. 1991. HortTechnology and the developing countries. *Horttechnology* (Oct/Dec):136–137.

Kader, A. A. 1983. Postharvest quality maintenance of fruits and vegetables in developing countries. In *Postharvest Physiology and Crop Preservation*, ed. M. Lieberman, pp. 520–536. New York: Plenum.

Kader, A. A. 1992. Postharvest technology of horticultural crops. Publication 3311, 2nd ed., University of California, Davis.

Kat, J., and A. Diop. 1985. Manual on the establishment operation and management of cereal banks. Agricultural Services Bulletin 64. Rome: United Nations Food and Agriculture Organization.

Lancaster, P. A., and D. G. Coursey. 1984. Traditional post-harvest technology of perishable tropical staples. Agricultural Services Bulletin 59. Rome: United Nations Food and Agriculture Organization.

Lay-Yee, M., and K. J. Rose. 1994. Quality of Fantasia nectarines following forced air heat treatments for insect disinfestations. *HortScience* 27:1254–1255.

Lawn rollers. www.ohiosteel.com/roll.html

Lisa Kitinoja and Adel A. Kader, 2002. Small Scale Postharvest Handling Practices: A Manual for Horticultural Crops (4th edition). July 2002. University of California, Davis, Postharvest Technology Research and Information Center

McGregor, B. 1989. Tropical Products Transport Handbook. USDA, Office of Transportation, Agricultural Handbook Number 668.

Miller, W. M., J. K. Burns, & J. D. Whitney. 1995. Effects of harvesting practices on damage to Florida grapefruit & orange. Applied Engineering in Agriculture 11(2): 265-269 Description/

Parmar, C. 1991. Some Himalayan wild fruits worth trial elsewhere. Chronica Horticulturae 31(2):19–20.

Reid, M.S. 2002. In: Kader, A.A. (Ed.) Postharvest Technology of Horticultural Crops. University of California, Division of Agriculture and Natural Resources, Publication 3311.

Rice, R. P., L. W. Rice, and H. D. Tindall. 1987. *Fruit and Vegetable Production in Africa*. London: Macmillan.

Russell, D. C. 1969. Cashew Nut Processing. Agricultural Services Bulletin 6. Rome: United Nations Food and Agriculture Organization.

Solhjoo, K. 1994. Food technology and the Bahai Faith. *Food Science and Technology Today*, 8(1):2–3.

Thompson, A. K., 1996. *Postharvest Technology of Fruit and Vegetables*. Oxford: Blackwell.

Tow-Behind-Lawn-Sweeper.www.homedepot.com/p/John-Deere-42-in-24-cu-ft-Tow-Behind-Lawn-Sweeper-STS-42JD/100361705#.Uahln6DTSt8

Walker, D.J. (Ed) 1992. World Food Programme Food Storage Manual. Chatham, UK: Natural Resources Institute

------Wikipedia, the free encyclopedia.htm

Wood, B.W., and J. A. Payne. 1991. Pecan: An emerging crop. Chronica Horticulturae 31(2):21–23.

Titles in author's list

The book gave an overview of agricultural engineering fundamentals, which is does not adequately represent some aspects of field practice in engineering training in our University, Polytechnic and Colleges curricular. This Volume of the title series 'Agricultural Engineering principles & practice covers wider scope of agricultural engineering practice. Three major aspects of agricultural engineering were explored: Agricultural engineering development, Agricultural land preparation and Crop planting and establishment.

ISBN-13: 978-147-931-614-4
URL:https://www.createspace.com/3996235

Available
on-line

This Volume explores engineering involvement in soil and water conservation, agricultural material properties, processing and handling as well as farm structure requirement, farmstead layout, storage structures and construction, animal housing requirements among others. The book undoubtedly provides essential engineering fundamentals required by students for effective teaching and practical training in skill acquisition. The book is therefore recommended for all students of agricultural and engineering technology students in training at different levels in the university, polytechnic, colleges and vocational schools.

ISBN-13: 978-145-633-568-7
URL: https://www.createspace.com/3498612

Available on-line

This book provide an overview of the advances which have been made and are currently in progress to provide a strong base for a review of agricultural engineering curriculum in order to catch up with the global trend in agricultural engineering revolution especially in Nigeria. For the ever increasing population, the drudgeries involved in food production, incurable losses in harvest and post harvest operations as well as the ever increasing and increased expectation of high quality food products meeting consumers' need and satisfying food safety standards had called for the growth of accurate, fast and objective quality determination indices of agricultural and cost effective techniques employed in food production.

ISBN-13: 978-080-015-8

Available in
bookstores

The dynamic nature of agricultural operations and the complexity of agricultural machinery are indices of scientific research diversity as evident in the wide spread requirements in agricultural operation sustainable production. Engr. Segun presents extensive works on agricultural mechanization and machinery utilization in agricultural production documented in this eleven chapter book to acquaint students and researchers with the principles of agricultural machinery and provide them with requisite knowledge and skills on various agricultural machinery requirements for effective agricultural mechanization.

ISBN-13: 978-145-632-876-4.
URL: https://www.createspace.com/3497673

Available
on-line

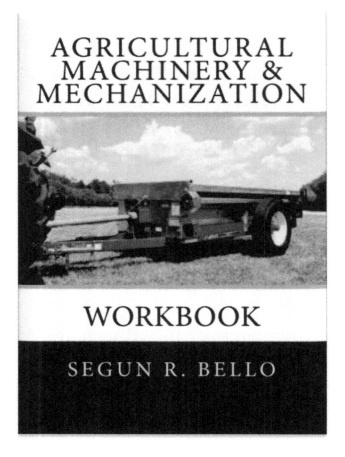

The author designs this workbook to help students have an understanding of the practical content of the agricultural machinery as a course and to guide them in carrying out determination of mechanization indicators, machine performance indices and also field experimentation, monitoring and reporting to improve the quality of practical presentation and documentation to meet the requirements of NBTE, NUC and other examination bodies. The workbook directly improves students' opportunity to learn new concepts of log entry and field measurement and computation by direct participation, acceptance of new methodology from instructors, and breeding of future technicians.

ISBN-13: 978- 1484927038
         - 1484927036
URL:https://www.createspace.com/4277084

Available
on-line

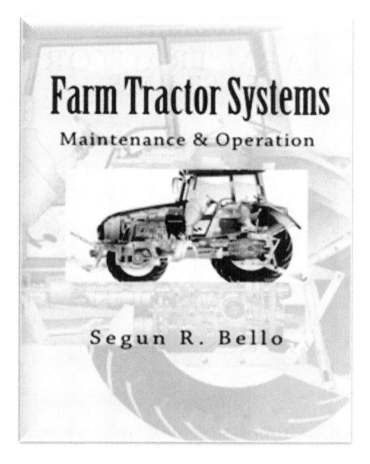

A link between machine functionality, operations, performance and decision making in the management of power sources and field operations were presented in this book. Depreciation and functional deviation of a machine from its original state at manufacture could put the life of a machine in danger of breakdown or obsolescence, which is counted a loss to any such organization or the entrepreneur. To avoid such losses, an understanding of machine systems functionality and a well organized maintenance programme designed to maintain, prevent or restore machine to near original state is required.

ISBN-13: 978-148-102-292-7
URL:https://www.createspace.com/3996235

Available on-line

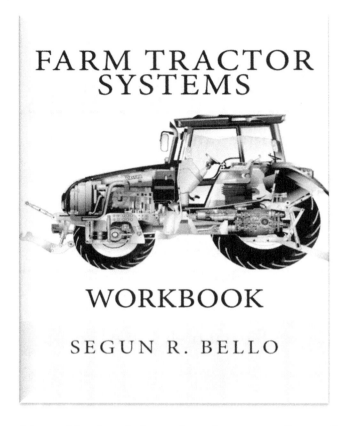

The author designs this workbook to help students have an understanding of the practical contents of the farm tractor and to guide them in carrying out system maintenance, repairs, overhauling and engine tune-up as well as reporting field experimentation and monitoring. This is in effort to improve the quality of practical presentation and documentation in order to add value to quality. The practical exercises improve students' opportunity to learn new concepts by direct participation, acceptance of new material from instructors, and breeding of future technicians.

ISBN-13: 978-148-491-835-7

URL:https://www.createspace.com/4272459

Available on-line

This book is all you need in emergency breakdown and where there is no mechanic. It offers a guide to decision making in machinery procurement, farm power selection, engine troubleshooting, tractor driving and operations as well as tractor and machinery maintenance and repairs. In this way, the enormous costs and valuable time spent on waiting desperately at breakdown points, tracing of faults, annoying breakdowns, unnecessary down time and costly repairs can be adequately reduced.

ISBN-13: 978-332-254-4-3

Available in bookstores

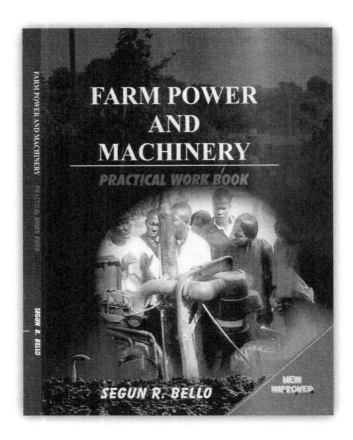

This Practical workbook is an expression of the student's desire to have a simplified extraction from the practical content of the topics discussed in my previous work; Guide to Agricultural Machinery Maintenance and Operations. There is urgent need for students to learn the art of presentation of technical report through active participation and reporting. This workbook present a simple approach to achieving such objective than it had been in the past. With the contents of this workbook, it is easier to follow laid down procedures to carry out practicals, and report them appropriately. Conducting, reporting and documentation of students' practical activities therefore become easier and more presentable.

ISBN-13: 978-376-67-1-6

Available in bookstores

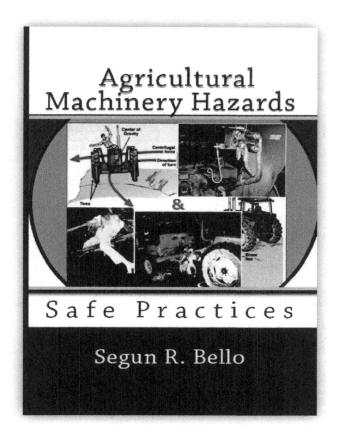

As long as agriculture underpins the survival of humanity, safety remains a relevant issue to life security in and around the farm community for system sustainability. An understanding of the issues and values of hazard and safety in machinery operations as presented in this book with *full coloured graphic prints* will aid in decision-making reinforced by principles and practice as well as facilitate effective utilization of signal communication techniques and the attainment of relevant knowledge in accident prevention in primary production processes.

ISBN-13: 978-146-790-718-7
URL:https://www.createspace.com/3498621

Available
on-line in
full colour

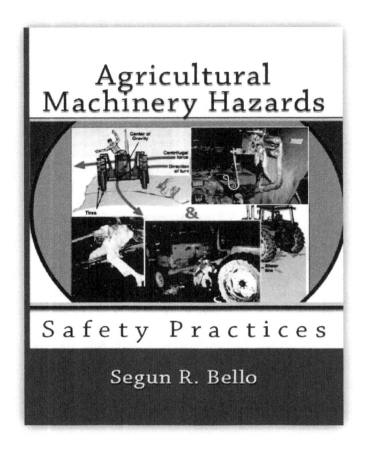

The diversity and complexity of agricultural and related machinery have become an index for increased rate of accident and injury occurrence experienced during operations and maintenance. Therefore, the study of machinery hazards, hazard sources and points in machinery and subsequent safe practices will help to eliminate, eradicate or control such hazards and provide workers with the opportunity to operate machinery more safely and develop skills in improved material and machine handling, as well as facilitate effective utilization of signal communication techniques and the attainment of relevant knowledge in accident prevention in primary production processes.

ISBN-13: 978-147-753-664-3
URL: https://www.createspace.com/3728177

Available
on-line in
black & white

In as much as we live within hazardous environments, it is our responsibility to make the environment favourable. It is our responsibility to provide guide to workers' safety, change attitude and offer safety training programmes to ensure safe work environment. Remember, it is important to make rules about safety; however, it is more important to ensure safety by locking dangers away. This book x-rays the various workplaces and associated hazards as well as provides an insight to some measures of safety within workplace.

ISBN-13: 978-147-528-554-3.

https://www.createspace.com/3865653

Available
on-line

This book is designed to help students acquire requisite knowledge and skills in basic workshop technologies & practices, workshop management, organization and handling of tools and machines in preparations to meet the demands of the manufacturing and processing sector of our economy. The author believed that reading through this book, users will be able to appreciate the work environment and the influences it has on the workers' safety and as well have gained enough experience that will guide you in safe tool handling and machine operation which guarantees effective job delivery without incidences of hazards, injury or accident.

ISBN-13: 978-147-928-308-8
URL: https://www.createspace.com/3982311

Available
on-line

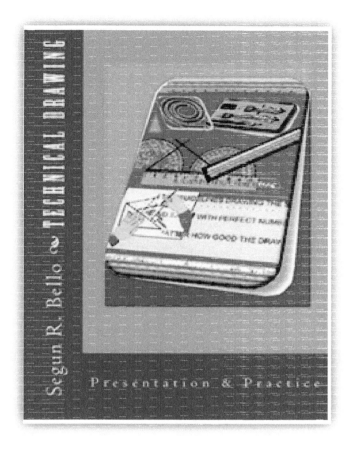

This book was packaged to help students acquire requisite knowledge and practical skills in engineering/technical drawing practices. The contents were designed to prepare students for technical, diploma and degree examinations in engineering, engineering technology and technical vocations in other professions in the monotechnics, polytechnics and universities. Emphasis is placed on media drafting, lettering, and alphabet of lines, geometric construction, sketching, and multiview drawings.

ISBN-13: 978-148-125-012-2
URL:https://www.createspace.com/3996235

Available
on-line

This book is written to provide the students with a good understanding in fruits and vegetables handling, processing, and technological advances in preservation of fruits and vegetable from harvest t.ill it gets to the consumer table or ended at the store shelf as finished products. Fruits and vegetables surfers the highest degree of deterioration at all levels of technological involvement right from maturity till shelving. This book is therefore packaged to advance knowledge and increase understanding of the nature of the fruits and vegetables in order to match up the principles and techniques of crops handling, processing and storage in order to minimize post harvest losses.

ISBN-13: 978- 149-047-910-1
    -10: 149-047-910-4
URL:https://www.createspace.com/

Available on-line

HORTICULTURAL
MACHINERY

OPERATIONS & SAFETY

SEGUN R. BELLO

This book is packaged to provide the students with background knowledge of various horticultural operations, tool and equipment use. Written in simplified English with detailed graphic illustrations and pictures, the book is the perfect tool required in every home to in selecting tools and machines for horticultural and gardening operations.

ISBN-13: 978- 148-497-487-2
   -10: 148-497-487-5
URL:https://www.createspace.com/4284225

Available
on-line

The author designs this workbook to help students have an understanding of the practical content of the horticultural machinery course and to guide them in reporting field experimentation and monitoring. This is in effort to improve the quality of practical presentation and documentation in order to add value to quality of practical as well as improve students' opportunity to learn new concepts by direct participation, acceptance of new instructional materials, and breeding of future technicians.

ISBN-13: 978-148-492-821-9

-148-492-821-0

URL:https://www.createspace.com/4277259

Available in online bookstores

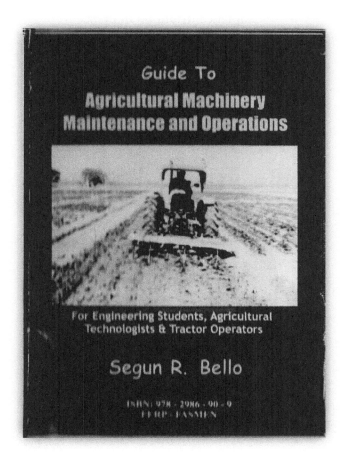

This manual is prepared to provide an essential guide to students' practical in agricultural engineering and agricultural technology programmes and also at appropriate levels in other tertiary institutions in the country. In preparing the manual, the requirements and minimum standards specified by the various academic regulatory bodies in Nigeria such as: National Board for Technical Education (NBTE), Nigeria Universities Commission (NUC) Nigeria Society of Engineers (NSE), National Commission for Colleges of Education (NCCE), Council for the Regulation of Engineering in Nigeria (COREN) etc, were taken into consideration.

ISBN-13: 978-298-6-90-9

Available in bookstores

Chapter contribution in Books

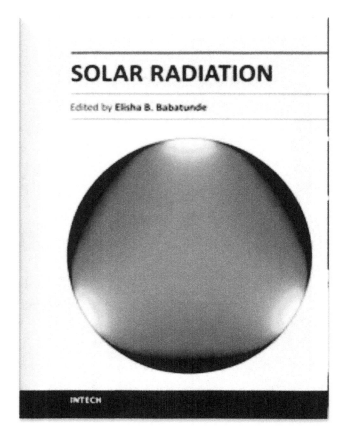

The book presents fundamental and well researched contributions on possible, feasible and future applications of solar radiation as an energy source by world class scientists including the author. As old as its source, the sun, little did the world knew of its potential as an enormous energy provider. It has now attracted the attention of scientists, engineers and even the public and attracted the attention of the academic curricula of science and engineering courses in higher institutions. It is studied as an environmental science and as an energy course, particularly in the aspect of alternative or renewable energy source both in science and engineering departments of universities.

ISBN: 978-953-51-0384-4.

http://www.intechopen.com/books/solar-radiation

Available
on-line

Edited books

Sustainability of agricultural production system is becoming a major concern to agricultural research and policy makers in both developed and developing countries as it represents the last step in a long evolution of the protection of natural resources and the maintenance of environmental quality. This 6-part book furnish scientists and students with fundamental views on scientific developments, research outcome on sustainable solutions and also offers guidance on dissemination of sustainable agricultural techniques and feasible applications to Nigeria situation as a way of wriggling out of the ever expensive, environmentally degrading conventional machine and inorganic agricultural production practices.

ISBN-13: 978-148-010-344-3

URL: https://www.createspace.com/4025911

Available on-line

For more information, visit:

1. http://www.amazon.com/Segun-R.-Bello/e/B008AL6RI0
2. http://www.amazon.com/s?ie=UTF8&field-author=Engr%20Segun%20R.%20Bello&page=1&rh=n%3A283155%2Cp_27%3AEngr%20Segun%20R.%20Bello
3. http://www.amazon.com/Segun-R.-Bello/e/B008AL6RI0
   http://www.amazon.com/s?ie=UTF8&field-author/
4. http://lejpt.academicdirect.org/
5. http://www.cigr-ejournal.tamu.edu/
6. http://www.intechopen.com/books/solar-radiation
7. http://www.medwelljournals
8. http://www.sciacademypublisher.com/journals/index.php/SATRESET

THE HEXAGON-LANCASTER
AND MORECAMBE COLLEGE

Lightning Source UK Ltd.
Milton Keynes UK
UKOW07f1915290416

273255UK00005B/54/P

When I Was Little Like You

PUFFIN BOOKS

Published by the Penguin Group
Penguin Books Ltd, 27 Wrights Lane, London W8 5TZ, England
Penguin Putnam Inc., 375 Hudson Street, New York, New York 10014, USA
Penguin Books Australia Ltd, Ringwood, Victoria, Australia
Penguin Books Canada Ltd, 10 Alcorn Avenue, Toronto, Ontario, Canada M4V 3B2
Penguin Books (NZ) Ltd, 182–190 Wairau Road, Auckland 10, New Zealand

Penguin Books Ltd, Registered Offices: Harmondsworth, Middlesex, England

First published by Viking 1997
Published in Puffin Books 1998
3 5 7 9 10 8 6 4 2

Text copyright © Jill Paton Walsh, 1997
Illustrations copyright © Stephen Lambert, 1997

The moral right of the author and illustrator has been asserted

Made and printed in Italy by printers srl – Trento

British Library Cataloguing in Publication Data
A CIP catalogue record for this book is available from the British Library

ISBN 0-140-55829-2

When I Was Little Like You

Jill Paton Walsh

Illustrated by
Stephen Lambert

PUFFIN BOOKS

"Look, Gran," said Rosie.
"Look at the train, Gran."

"When I was little like you," said Gran, "a steam engine pulled the carriages. It made little home-made clouds as it puffed round the headland."

"Look, Gran," said Rosie.
"Look at the ice-cream van."

"When I was little like you," said Gran, "the ice-cream seller was a man on a bicycle. He had a sign that said 'Stop me and Buy One'."

"Look, Gran," said Rosie.
"Look at the boats, Gran."

"When I was little like you," said Gran, "the boats had brown sails, not engines. They couldn't get out of the harbour unless the wind would let them."

"Look, Gran," said Rosie.
"Look at the fish shop, Gran."

Closed

"When I was little like you," said Gran, "we bought fish from the boatmen on the quay. A brace of bright mackerel for supper, still fresh and shining."

"Look, Gran," said Rosie.
"Look at the sweets, Gran."

"When I was little like you," said Gran, "the sweets were in rows of glass bottles. We bought them at four for a penny, or one for a farthing."

"Look, Gran," said Rosie.
"Look at the surfers, Gran."

"When I was little like you," said
Gran, "nobody knew how to do that.
When the waves were wild we played
catch-as-catch-can with the breakers."

"Look, Gran," said Rosie.
"Look at the lighthouse, Gran."

"When I was little like you," said Gran, "the lighthouse looked just like that on fine summer evenings."

"Did you like the world better, Gran, the way it was when you were little like me?"

"Oh no, my dear, no! The world is more fun by far now it has you in it!"